Praise for *New Singapore Poetries*

"An overwhelming collection, each voice is singular, every page yields surprises. One is no longer certain where the boundaries are in the bounty of talents. True to the spirit of Gaudy Boy, an exciting poetry enterprise that enlarges one's vision of Singapore."

—Wong May, author of
In the Same Light: 200 Tang Poems for our Century

"Ally Chua's "The boys in the Lineup" stands out as a kind of poem-blurb for *New Singapore Poetries*, an editorially policed line-up of suspects all guilty, in one way and another, of indecency, disrespect, transgression—and crucial originality. The politics—post-colonial, ecological, sexual—are vividly embodied in psalms, visual poems, elegies, sequences, satires. Jack Xi's sequence on the McDonald burger is just one riveting exercise in making the world real in verse. Lines from other poems stay in memory, "the only thing complicated is vegetables" (Kenneth Constance Loe) and "I hear her say/*come, let us be fish*" (Laetitia Keok); in Singapore are figured the cities, past and present, of the world. Marylyn Tan quarries her poems out of ancient material (Christ's prepuce) and modern (the language of sex sites) to great effect. The book is full of surprise, offence, humour and, above all, unexpected pleasure. The English language is re-energised by its unblushing encounters with a specific set of contemporary worlds."

—Michael Schmidt, editor of
Carcanet's *New Poetries* and of *PN Review*

"The word 'renaissance' has been used to describe the unprecedented emergence of poets in 1990s Singapore. There is ample evidence in this compelling gathering of young poets to suggest that another renaissance is happening, one that is more varied, diverse in gender, race and culture, more bold and adventurous in poetics and politics. Reading these poems one is struck by the astonishing array of distinct, arresting voices and styles, the poets' attentiveness to words and the in-between spaces, their readiness to push the boundaries of form and technique, and the quest to be free of the shackles of identity politics, to explore and extend the possibilities of what it means to be Singaporean and a poet in these challenging, fast-changing times."

—Boey Kim Cheng, author of
The Singer and Other Poems

"Hoa Nguyen's "Poem" talks about poems as "potential to create without/possession" and that poems also unbind reference. *New Singapore Poetries* challenges us to question and unsettle known tropes, to leave one shore of definitions in search of other possible meanings. The poets featured in this anthology are varied in their styles, subject matter and poetics; some include the use of other languages to unbind us from habitual reliance on a colonial legacy and to centre instead their vital cultural experiences. Others dismantle the normative through queer subversions and investigations. We the readers are treated to a sumptuous palette of fresh linguistic exploration."

—Lydia Kwa, author of *Pulse* and *sinuous*

"Loud, proud and unbowed—there's *a lot* to plumb in *New Singapore Poetries*, a cornucopia of young and emerging poetic voices spiked with vigour, rudeness, melodrama and devil-may-care sass. To steal a line from Hamid Roslan, these poems defy the essentialist death-trap: "Where I am taught how I ought to see myself." Instead, these truth-seekers strive for a spirited un-learning, a delicious abandonment of old, didactic ways. Making something (themselves) new, they demand to be judged on their own terms, warts and all. Whether conjuring highly personalised, inter-lingual hinterlands, or zooming in on cycles of animalia and machinery, they navigate intersections of identity and gender and community with strange interest."

—Yeow Kai Chai, author of
One to the Dark Tower Comes

"Vital, form-busting gorgeousity made flesh ... *New Singapore Poetries* breaks—and makes—new ground with the ardency and agency of these fresh voices."

—Amanda Lee Koe, author of
Ministry of Moral Panic

"Jammed into this anthology are the fiercest and the gentlest emotions from a new age of Singaporean poets. Their range attests to a startling flamboyance racing from madcap sweeps of history to urgent violations of thoughts on form, feeling, and the sublime. Here is poetry post-tradition enough to know that there is still a lot of fun to be had!"

—Gwee Li Sui, poet, graphic artist, literary critic

"In this anthology, blood ripens into honey, prayer takes the shape of a lurching metronome and poems leave footprints in flour. A striking and original collection."

—Tania de Rozario, author of
And the Walls Come Crumbling Down

"Skeptical of sentiment and yet full of feeling, these poems are built not out of tired angsana trees and the weary merlions but of this new conglomeration of form and discontent, desire and humour and dare I say joy, or a version of it, that makes me want to say more, more!"

—Lawrence Lacambra Ypil, author of
The Experiment of the Tropics

"Undeniably one of the world's great metropolises, Singapore's Anglophone poetry hasn't received nearly as much attention as it so evidently deserves, and this first-rate anthology effectively helps to remedy that state of affairs, introducing us to work that is passionate, sardonic, cosmopolitan and conversant in the city-state's multiple and layered identities, adroitly spilling out of the island's physical confines to set its ambitious sights on the whole world."

—André Naffis-Sahely, editor of *Poetry London*

NEW
SINGAPORE
POETRIES

NEW SINGAPORE POETRIES

POEMS BY
ALLY CHUA, ANDREW KIRKROSE DEVADASON,
ANURAK SAELAOW, CHRISTIAN YEO, HAMID ROSLAN,
ILA, IZYANTI ASA'ARI, JACK XI,
KENNETH CONSTANCE LOE, LAETITIA KEOK,
LISABELLE TAY, LUNE LOH, MARYLYN TAN,
MOK ZINING, NATHANIEL CHEW, SHAWN HOO,
SHOU JIE ENG, WORMS VIRK

EDITED BY
MARYLYN TAN AND JEE LEONG KOH

Collection copyright © 2022 Marylyn Tan, Jee Leong Koh

Editor's introduction copyright © 2022 Marylyn Tan

Text copyright individual contributors.
Permissions are on pages 295–297.

Published by Gaudy Boy LLC,
an imprint of Singapore Unbound
www.singaporeunbound.org/gaudyboy
New York

For more information on ordering books, contact jkoh@singaporeunbound.org.

All rights reserved. No part of this publication may be reproduced or transmitted in any form or by any means without the prior written permission of the publisher, except for brief excerpts for the purpose of criticism and review.

ISBN 978-0-9994514-9-6

Cover design by Flora Chan
Interior design by Jennifer Houle

CONTENTS

Editor's Introduction by Marylyn Tan   xi

ILA

seni itu sunyi	1
Diam-Diam	3
Hari Kebangsatan	4
Pura-Pura Parade: murni, Bebean, Drone dreamers, Priscilla the German Girl	5

ANURAK SAELAOW

Executive Summary	11
Degustation	12
Affidavit Disregarding the Body	13
Concerning Anurak	15
Strategic Sand Reserves	17
Matt Berninger, Distracted, Speaks to GQ	21
Bat Bridge (. . . [Begat Bird])	23
Bat Bridge (Self-Portrait as Self-Portrait in a Convex Mirror)	24

LISABELLE TAY

Mangosteen Season	29
John at the end of his days	30
Solarium	31
On the Curative Properties of Incense	32
Pilgrim	33
Psalm of Prey	34
Three Stars	36
Self-portrait as a moirologist	37

NATHANIEL CHEW

language acquisition	41
set for a litany	42
oologies: two and a half perspectives	43
litany for a pantry	44
language remission	48
scar story	49
pattern recognition	50
rag / bone	51
after eschatology	52
language death	53

KENNETH CONSTANCE LOE

equilibrium for a hot minute;	57
An embarrassment to embalm	59
strangely comeuppance,	60
Alaska	61
it starts with a nip,	62
how many potential beaux does it take to change a fennel bulb?	63
not a number	64
you can only break a stem with your bare hands if it's dry	65
There is a chain that lies beyond daisies	66
Laeken Placid	67
Pitahaya in Three Parts	69

JACK XI

This Solidity, Of Course, Is What Humankind Yearns For	73
A Season of Slime	74
La Malekzorcismo de la Kvira Korpo	76
The Feelings of Old Woman Lee	78
In the Guts of Your Mooncake an Egg	80
A Lot Like Ourselves	81
The Merman Dye and Another Man Talking	92
The Purpose of Fruit	93

MOK ZINING

Floristry Basics: Cuttings	97
Floristry Basics: Synonyms	98
Exemplary Arrangement C: "Colonialism: Adaptive Reuse"	99
Lesson on Cuttings: Trimming Unnecessary Affixes	100
Exemplary Arrangement C: Background & Discussion Questions	102
Bestselling Bouquets: Vanda Miss Joaquim Pendant	103
Orchid Basics: Lip Modification	104

LAETITIA KEOK

Grief Work	107
The Rivers of Us	111
Etymology of My Mother	115
The Lovers Become Butterflies	116
In Defense of My Grandmother's Bittergourd Soup	117
Maxwell Food Centre (1997)	119
Object Permanence	121

WORMS VIRK

20 August 2019, 9.03 p.m.	125
The body is a temple	128
He Fucked Me Like the North-South Line	131
Lockdown Fucking	135

ALLY CHUA

Pedigree	139
Juxtaposition of apron strings	140
Martin Scorsese and I Get into a Taxi	141
It happened again—	147
lunar cycle	149
The Boys in the Lineup	151

SHAWN HOO

Natural History of the Florids, 19th Century	157
Natural History of the Florids, 20th Century	161
Natural History of the Florids, 21st Century	165
Deferred Sayings for the Next Century	170
There	171
You Want to Write a Sentence as Clean as a Bone	172
Placard	173
Ode to the Public Toilet	174

IZYANTI ASA'ARI

Rubik's mess	179
Parting words	180
After the mountain	182
In the desert, a wolf	183
Crease	184
The boulder that swallows you	185
The city has a request	187
Doorway	188
The horizon bends	189

LUNE LOH

I WAS BLUR AND FORGOT WHEN MY ASSIGNMENT WENT	193
Left Breast (Take 1 - Take 5)	194
x1 Right-Breast-Pad (Pinkish, Silicone, Attached)	195
Breath as Cinema	196
FEMME DIALECTICS: A PROCESS	197
Sleep Paralysis as Lucid Dreaming	198
Mall World	199
Mood as Spacetime Errata Pt. 2	200

SHOU JIE ENG

Eight Divers	203
Mirabilis	211
How We Build (When We Know How)	212

CHRISTIAN YEO

Refuge	217
Colonial Apologist	218
Bath Towel Sits at the Intersection of Two Chairs	219
After Me	220
What Is Masculinity But Adolescence Without End?	221
Grace	222
Farm Mart	223
Miles	224

ANDREW KIRKROSE DEVADASON

INTERLOPER *says*	227
GLASS VASE CELLO CASE	228
preparation for / cleansing the blood	229
Excerpt from "The Spare Parts Cycle"	230
TRUTH CONDITIONS	233
THIS BLENDER GRINDS THE MEAT	234
seed	236
in endless iteration	237
seventeen	238
WHY ARE YOU STILL LYING AT THE WEIGHING OF THE HEART?	239
Sympathetic Resonance	242

MARYLYN TAN

daddy issues	245
A WET CRIMSON BUSHEL OF PEARS	248
THE OSCAR ROSARY—THE DEDICATION, LITANY OF OUR OSCAR AS TRAGIC GAY ICON THIS IS HOW TO SLAUGHTER A BIRD YOU OBTAIN FROM THE MARKET	249
QUEER FILTH INFERNAL	255
CURSING THE FIG TREE	257
tagged 'singapore'	264

HAMID ROSLAN

The Shape of a Body Uncertain   269

About the Poets   289
About the Editors   293
Permissions   295
About Gaudy Boy   299

EDITOR'S INTRODUCTION

In carving out space and creating the ideal conditions under which new work will flourish, one inevitably finds oneself reckoning with how to best curate and display something burgeoning, something nascent. *New Singapore Poetries* is an ambitious attempt to platform the newest poetic voices of Singapore, who speak both tenderly and critically of it, who provide perspectives with a freshness and conviction we have been so eager to see.

It is the editors' hopes that this anthology of emerging poets, each with not more than a single volume of poetry published, will nourish and agitate a growing movement towards a poetics that is both inventive and considered in its choices. Selfishly, I wanted to be excited about poetry again. I wanted to see us peel apart from homogeneity and an imaginary standard of what makes for a *good* poem, *good* meaning acceptable, meaning palatable, meaning easily digestible, meaning decent, meaning respectable, meaning *safe*. As such, I was heartened and mollified to discover some gorgeously bold, brash, and invitingly strange voices in our midst.

New Singapore Poetries comprises poets who each attend to their craft with precision and discernment. It is a point of great pleasure to be able to witness the way form and content are deconstructed and repurposed, deviating from what, even, a poem is often considered to be. The *newness* of these poetries, then, lies in them chasing a throughline to what is important, paying attention to the keenness of their concerns, and then presenting them in forms varied and ever-evolving—archival documentation, visual art, experiments with breath, placement, and sound.

Despite such a variety of intensely diverse concerns and voices, there are strong recurring themes discernible in the collection—fractured relationships with family, for instance, reckoning with the self, the body, sexuality, histories and geographies both present and erased, colonialism, tradition, religion. It is a collection both tactile and cerebral, where Kenneth Constance Loe's queer clusterfuck feasting ("this glossolalia of abominable scents. / Instead visual enters your nostrils, shoving", *Alaska*) curls itself up next to Mok Zining's clinicality-with-a-flourish ("where, if my bones must remain in the East, they would have the honour of mixing with the ashes of the Malayan kings", *Lesson on Cuttings: Trimming Unnecessary Affixes*), which in turn nuzzles towards Hamid Roslan's stark, exacting eye ("resent this body / its acre of feelings / false measure / legal fiction", *The Shape of a Body Uncertain*).

An additional note about this diversity—in such glorious company, one sometimes feels a little discomfited. At first, I wondered about the propriety of including of my own work and the work of a few other Singapore Unbound/Gaudy Boy team members in this anthology, but after much deliberation with my co-editor, Jee, and the Singapore Unbound team, we eventually returned to our original purpose of publishing such an anthology in the first place. The work included here is deemed both necessary and worthwhile in presenting the vision of *New Singapore Poetries* that we imagined.

The anthology begins with ila's discourses on art-making, race and racism, and how tradition jostles uneasily against the present, in itself a linguistic commentary on neo-colonialism. Post-nationalism, postpartum, post-heavinesses of identity and cultural dissociation, are we just left with our attention to the little things: "huat kueh / and defridged oranges" (Lisabelle Tay, *On the Curative Properties of Incense*), "the jelly tailed in umbilicus" (Jack Xi, *La Malekzorcismo de la Kvira Korpo*), "four molars / or a clump of hair" (Ally Chua, *It happened again—*)?

"The email says ANURAK you have won / great prizes. I am not looking for great prizes" (Anurak Saelaow, *Degustation*). Like Anurak, I am not looking for great prizes; I am sitting with an ear to the tide, looking for tiny crustaceans, still *here*, in a place resistant somehow to the reach of time. Even as Singapore bemoans its unending pursuit of progress with bitter wistfulness and not merely a hint of pride, poetry is a bulwark against the mad rush of capitalism, a moment crystalline, reflecting the present off its facets.

These poets straddle national identity and personal grief; process loss of history and rewritten trajectories; interrogate dialectics, boundaries, official narratives; traverse the sensuous and the sterile, the pleasurable and the austere, the natural world and natural language; and tell slanted the truth about the way our beloved and accursed country navigates such essentials as neo-liberalism, consumerism, and colonialism. It is our hope then that they will speak to you in a way that is both familiar and alien, making space for our desire to be heard and our thirst for an old truth spoken in a new way.

Newly yours,
Marylyn Tan

NEW
SINGAPORE
POETRIES

ILA

SENI ITU SUNYI

seni itu berat
seni itu sarat
seni itu lembik
hanya tahu ambik
tak pernah bagi
seni sudah basi
seni itu pedih
seni itu sedih
seni itu hilang
seni itu bayang
tidak bertulang
tidak berisi
seni itu janji
yang tak ditepati
seni itu suci
hanya dalam mimpi

seni banyak lobang
takut tunjuk belang
tapi tetap perahhh
macam pergi perang
dengan naluri
sampai kering kontang
seni itu harus,
harus bagi mati
seni, seni itu sunyi

seni itu v
suka nah melarat
seni itu parah
bagi orang marah
seni itu lapar
buat naik darah
buat kocek kosong
banyak berbual, banyak bohong
bikin hilang sabar

seni itu suci
hanya dalam mimpi
seni itu jiwang
seni itu sayang
seni kurang ajar
hahahahahaha
seni yang beradap
takut nak biadap
tapikan,
seni memang setan
buat hilang kawan
buat banyak musuh
seni tak kukuh
seni itu cinta
tapi cinta itu buta
seni, seni itu sunyi

seni makin berat
oh sudah tak larat
seni itu sombong
buat jiwa kosong
seni itu bodek
sampai tercekik
baru boleh naik
seni suka panjat
janganlah terperanjat
seni itu dengki
mari buat lagi
seni itu songsang
tak pernah kenyang
tak pernah cukup
buat aku takut
seni itu rugi
yang tak boleh ganti
hanya nak bertambah
tapi untuk siapa
cuma untuk aku
seni, seni itu sunyi

DIAM-DIAM

lapan baris tidak cukup untuk menerangkan gelap mendadak di ruang

sempit yang menggentel masa mengecil terselit di celahan gigiku yang lama reput dan nafasku yang

tersangkut di antara kertas tipis dan kuman naik angin. lapan baris tidak cukup untuk aku

merapikan ronyok isiku yang berkucar kacir di dalam pelukan masa depan yang tercicir

entahlah dekat mana sambil aku meraba-raba jatuh tergolek terseret gerun yang membisik

manja di kuping telingaku. mungkin lapan baris ini cukup sahaja buat sekarang

karang untuk diam diam seperti batu yang melihat semuanya walaupun tidak bermata.

HARI KEBANGSATAN

Memang sajak pun that national day this year falls at the start of the Hungry Ghost Festival. Burning money, hell notes, duit to satiate the hunger of dead ancestors. Nenek moyang aku dah lama kena tanam, diam diam dalam tanah. We are told to watch what we step on, be careful not to kick any offerings, jangan langkah sembarangan, careful as how we are taught to keep our mouths shut jadi hantu tak ikut balek. 56 years of kebangsaan. Kau tahu the word race can only be translated to perlumbaan on Google and the closest equivalent to that is bangsa, kebangsaan, nationality, bangsa, bangsa, bangsat. The Malay word for racist is its anglicised version, rasis. Jadi aku jaga langkah tak mahu langgar because we all know nothing good comes of pot stirring, boat rocking, just stating the obvious, shhh jangan teguh. And as these half-burnt hell notes takes up three quarters of the pavement and I tiptoe through this mess, I am not allowed to turn away even though I can never speak about it even if I try. As these papers fly about cinders in the air, burning in my throat and mata aku pedih tak boleh tutup, aku janji aku takkan tegur, teguh, aku dah lemau malas tak kuasa, tak berkuasa lupa kan sahaja.

PURA-PURA PARADE

Pura-Pura Parade is a series of flash prose pieces with sci-fi, spiritualism, and speculative elements

murni

the words move like the winds of horses, warm breaths on the ubun-ubun—the fontanelle. I always believed that's where memories of past lives cling to, and as it hardens, around seven months later, we forget who we were before. I closed my eyes and let the words run, fast and blindly inside.

sugeng rawuh paro simbah sesepuh, niat ingsun manjing I giant kulo si jabang bayinye murni.

"murni, you know girls can't ride. your semangat is not strong enough. you'll fall sick. you need to have a semangat of men, as strong as saints. don't be stubborn, murni."

murni means pure or clean. I was named after my great grandmother who passed away when I was two. she used to make these horses by hand, nine each time: Malek, Ampel, Giri, Bonang, Drajat, Kudus, Kaligaja, Muria, Jati. I mouthed their names again and again, pairing it with mine. the nine saints and I, until I could feel my feet tremble with impatience.

badhe ngundang sang hiyang moyo kakang kawah adi ari papat jejer kalimo pancer ingsun.

in this world, we treat animals as lesser beings, subjugated for our benefit, reared, poached, consumed, killed. in the liminal, there is no possession, no control, no power, but all the power is in us as we dance and resist the realities of this world. I am the horses, the saints, the spirits of the nameless am I. in the liminal, there is no such thing as weakness or strength because you are both. "murni, don't be stubborn. we follow traditions. this is how things have been for the longest time. there was never a female saint because we are not worthy, sayang." I smiled to myself. but all these saints were birthed by women, mak.

Bebean

The lush green fields are tropical mirages that seemed to mock at the starving folk; eyes wide and searching, desperately hungry from weeks of rationed stock that have been stretched and began grow as thin as their gaunt skin and flesh. Crops that survived the harvest were not edible. I imagined ugliness spilling itself out in times like these, but it has made us humble and soft, mirroring the old days of farmers as if they were at the mercy of the divine. The winds were strong, but the crops did not yield. This was the last desperate measure of an offering. "Shiva's wrath has fallen on us all, you can feel it in your bones," he said as he attempted to fly the poorly made bebean skywards, hampered by the countless plunges unto the barren ground. The spinning string vibrated precariously, staccatos of screams, high pitch and shrill, so vastly different from the low drone humming of a time long gone. "Now you can hear it too," he said with resignation in his voice.

Drone dreamers

The survivors are calling it the absence, the deterioration of the brain's ability to retain the past. The first obvious symptom is the cycling of a hyper-fugue state lasting weeks and gradually months. Lovers would wake up in their beds as strangers, children would walk aimlessly in the streets unclaimed by their parents who have forgotten that they were ever conceived. The fugue state is followed by drone-dreaming where millions of the infected occupy spaces of resource and consume everything in their paths, forcing us, the survivors into hiding. There was no way one can be protected from being marked by the absence, no possibility of escaping it, rendering us helpless, waiting for our turns.

I have imagined the end of times as fast and unforgiving. A prophetic calamity sweeping our sorry selves into extinction. Never realising that it has always been this slow arduous decay in the guise of the continuity of our existence. These are consequences of biotech diseases from the past escalating its way into the present. The earliest forms known as dementia, Alzheimer's, Parkinson's. Our hubris kept us from looking for a cure. It will not happen to me, it will not happen to us. Now it was too late to prevent the source of disintegration. No information could be retained long enough even if there was ever a possibility of finding one.

Drone dreamers would sway in polyrhythms into the endstage. Some of us have called it the dance of madness, the final expulsions of consciousness, of characters and habits, of any sense of self. We watched from elevated grounds and hiding spots, the exuberance of these synchronised gestures and manic swaying. Most of us looked away from the horror as they submerged themselves into the sea, bobbing up and down, as though they were fighting their own bodies to keep alive. Others like myself, could not turn away. Could not help but feel, no, it will not happen to me. It will not happen to us.

Priscilla the German Girl

Before I broke into little clusters of myself, I've always thought that every single living thing will leave this world intact. Out one body into another: a tree dies and it lives in a fish, and when that fish dies it lives in a newborn baby, breathing in air out of water for the first time, many times over. Reincarnation, to enter flesh again as a whole and out as whole. But we never truly know these things, do we? Not the ways in which we will die and the forms in which we will take in our next lives and how the cycle goes on and on until it is extinguished into a void and we become nothing.

I was running in the dark, wrapped in panic that feels so far away now. I must have tripped on a rock and I fell, turning into blooming violet strands that stretched outwards and inwards, bellowing against the perimeter of the island. When I died that night, I did not know I was dying and maybe the perplexity of the situation, the fear that had set me running in the first place, bore down on the vertical surge, compressing all my parts into a circuitous mess. I was pulled across the trees and rocks and my dear parents who have surrendered themselves and were no longer able to save me from any life I may have left clinging onto that old body that I've known so well.

And there I was, for a really long time caught in the in-between and I belonged to the island and all the life that sits within it. I was still attached to my body and I witnessed, from where I was scattered, the people who had worked for my father covering me in sand, placing flowers on the rot and praying over me. I felt the heat from their voices, their bodies. I could smell them like vibrations through the many orifices of this multi-body.

I became a guest, in the weaving of layers I was occupying, leaking, spilling but never truly still. There are conditions of being a guest of the multibody. Purba, entities that existed way before time or consciousness, thrives and holds the highest power. Sometimes parts of me would settle and merge into a wholeness that is not really complete. I call this the inhabition. When it becomes hospitable and I have completely settled in, there's an amputation from the multi-body and lupa will set in.

Over the years parts of me have stayed in the multi-body as an in-between. There's not many of us here. The in-between shelters those that the living on the island refuse to let go. I was kept alive by the people who had worked for my father and was adopted several times by others. They seem to think they are taking care of me and sometimes they want something in return. Those in the in-between can only be released through inhabition. I never knew why it was hard for inhabition to happen but I've acquired ways in which to thrive. Mostly through the traum of other living things in the form of krasib, songs of our past desires. Krasib can hurt us sometimes. When it is sent out too strongly, the island will heave in mourning. Purba's rage can make the island sick so we need to send out krasib with good intentions.

Once when I sent out a krasib for my old name, I was gifted instead a beautiful non-body made of plastic, a plastic doll that looked just like me. It sits on the shrine as a myth. A nameless German girl, a powerful being in the living world but here in the in-between I am almost nothing but always something more or not yet known.

The largest inhabition of myself took place not so long ago in the form of a female boar. I sent out a million krasib, wanting my name to be said again. A desire that had been burning so bright. The humans on the island named her Priscilla, so close to my real name that I could feel the ache of the futility of my attempts. Maybe one day, I could hear my name being called out once more. Maybe when it happens, I will never leave this place and I will live on infinitely in this multi-body of traum, in the songs of krasib, on the lips of strangers mouthing their desires. Or I might be blown out, extinguished into nothing and completely forgotten.

ANURAK
SAELAOW

EXECUTIVE SUMMARY

Grounded in Dallas he sees small crystals
meander onto tarmac. Thinkpad huffing

like a matte crow spilt across his lap.
Men have inspected the feathery

outline of his bones and let him past.
Nowadays he feels most like a transient squall.

Lurching loosely, the lightning-fork of now
hucked into his side for the longest time.

In hours like these he wants a better way to be.
Something to take the edge off the press

of his feet into ground, the way skin warps
too tight about his see-through frame.

Anurak: the sky's unraveled like an errant skein
knocked across the unswept floor.

How easily he slips into the Embraer's belly.
Husking himself in steel and LCD displays.

Air strains on both sides of the cabin wall.
Frisson of doors at the edge of blowing off.

DEGUSTATION

I woke up presuming my arm was a windsock.
I woke up floating outside the garden.

All the sous-chef needed was a common lexicon.
An aperitif for the loud and gangly-mouthed

lingering on the patio. I lock myself out constantly
on the patio. Or was that a verandah

I thought of, wrought, muscled into view?
I project the turning icon of a house.

I watch my lover calculate down-payments.
Numbers soften like semantic candlesticks

in gloom. At perfect liberty to slink away.
A terrier yaps at the dark in the dark.

I stir cheap coffee for the next morning.
I am a gusty singlet on the pole.

The email says *ANURAK you have won*
great prizes. I am not looking for great prizes.

AFFIDAVIT DISREGARDING THE BODY

And yes, Anurak, sex is boring.
But suppose in its writhing

a gnostic cadence—

some selfish conviction
      of the body

           as fulcrum

to a fuller universe.

As if sensation itself
were the crux:

      the self as waterspout

picking up boats, people—
swirling detritus

inside his belly

      until sodden meaning
tumbles out.

Not exactly flaneur
or roving eye,

      he swallows

           and swallows and swallows.

Leaving in the rind,
        the thorn, the live wire—

        feeling the way
each thing writhes or changes,

        the way each thing changes him.

CONCERNING ANURAK

After Bidart

As the undersigned: his name
nailing in place
the fixed edges
of his confession.

Capturing a still
of all that abstract fire
coursing around
his breath.

Confession the act
of defining himself
in the chalk circle
of his guilt.

*

You have written the throes of it before.

Guilty of abstraction
  as if abdicating the material,
   the creased bedsheet of the living

in favor of some vexed
  ascetic existence—sitting again in a séance
where you lean forward, tuning in

to a tongue
greased
with tones of fire.

*

Anurak, you are not the voice
spilling like marrow from a fracture.

Blood ripening into honey
until its syrup drowns the wound.

Inside its skin the plum bursts.
From its wound: a drip of vinegar.

*

Writing not to excavate but to heap more dirt onto the whole.

O burial mound sitting like a scab over his heart:

O edifice somehow tall or artful enough to matter:

O light sneaking in the edges as if by sleight of hand:

                            Litigate

*

Confession itself a motif laced into his life.

The face, never at ease,
       doused in acetic fire.

Vertiginous, at the edge of being discovered.
His tongue wedged inside its cache
       like some deep-rooted lichen.

Growing thick in an oily silence.
       Professing to himself: I am, I am, I am.

STRATEGIC SAND RESERVES

"Much of Singapore lies less than 50 feet above sea level. A third of the island sits around 16 feet above the water—low enough to give planners the jitters."
—New York Times article dated April 20, 2017

i.

Strange, then, for an island to fear
the pending swell of the sea,
a coming tide high enough to nix

all trace of a history. The curling
commas of beaches scribbled over
with a child's wayward hand.

From the jetty we watch the flares
arc, then scatter. Dark water
echoes their light, as if in warning,

oily streaks of red stretched out
across its surface like a sudden
grasping claw. Miles away,

huddled underneath tarps,
mounds of sand loom in wait.
I imagine stripping off and diving,

feeling the coarseness rasp
against my body. Between
my toes the nascent land sifts

and courses, shifting around
the shape of my form, yearns
to be poured into being.

ii.

From above a fringe of white coast surrounds
the island like a chalk outline, keeping

at bay the encroaching blue that laps
constantly at our ankles. From the jetty

I gaze into a puddle and find the garlanded,
wavering form of a distant uncle, his eyes

opaque in the brine. Even in darkness
his rough skin flaunts its burnish,

a constellation of marks from the furled sails
of another time. He surfaces and gurgles

like a buoy hauled inland. I lean in
and hear a voice like an ancestral foghorn:

Reclaim. I shiver like a Danish prince
even in the heat of the tropics, thinking

of the taste of saltwater filtered through
the collective mouth of a nation, a people

retching from the weight of the sea. The tip
of my uncle's nose is washed away.

iii.

Only half-waking, oceans away, do I
confront the coming depth. I dream
of scooping water off my father's face

as he lies ear-deep, buried in sand.
How he shakes and spits as brine
trickles in and the waves conduct

their slow march up the shore.
My hands are freshly raw, stinging
with salt, unable to peel back

the tide as it seeps into his nostrils,
the gasping sinkhole of his mouth.
Soon I glimpse pearly bubbles,

then nothing. Jerked awake, I think
of the haplessness of distance
and time, the years used and spent

like the rockets I once observed
arcing over water. My parents
encased in that steady accretion

while I bob like a lone beacon
in the Atlantic, roiling in bed,
flashing my signals back east.

iv.

To steady myself
I pour words
into dams of silt
to fortify them
like incantations:

granite basalt limestone sand
cement coral mangrove plan

minute month millennium
rope enough to un-vanish

stutter sea enough for sun
sun decade salt decade

Letters swirl on
this inky surface
like the urgent
refractions of flares
I fling to home:

sing and pour, father
sing and pour

not decade delay decay decode
but expand expand expand

v.

The water gazes on with the weight of eons. I squint but cannot tell if it is ever turning back.

MATT BERNINGER, DISTRACTED, SPEAKS TO GQ

"Whatever I mutter I mutter always to one twin
or the other. Every demo begins like this: with the rattle
of cubes in the glass, the flicker of a burr set
and quickly dislodged from the throat. Move
too far from the mic and the mix falls apart—
like wet newsprint mashed together in the rough

approximation of a man, as rough
and smeary in form as my prickly twin
refracted in the studio's glass. He stands apart
from the brassy backwash, the rattle
of the drum machine. He moves as I move,
paces at arm's length throughout the set

until I, wine-drunk, lose track of where the set
ends and the changing room—with its rough
velveteen seats—begins. I fumble to remove
the clip-on mic. I fail to tell one twin
from the other. I feel the cork rattle
inside the bottle. I suppose—apart

from that—that I must be fine. "Apart
from that" meaning, of course, the set
of all possibilities—that haphazard rattle
of every quark. Reality rendered in rough
particulate clouds, a litany of twin
helixes that twines or continues to move

further into the viscera. Each day I move
closer to the stage's edge, fingers spread apart
and pleading. In solos I ping-pong from twin
to twin, not ceasing until the set
is done. Every comedown is rough:
the skull bounces like a baby's rattle

shaken again and again. I prattle
on to my wife, beg her to remove
the plug of my head or scoop out that rough
and crumbling gelatin. It falls apart
inside the mold—refuses to set
neatly in its cavern behind twin

eye-sockets. Still: the rattled self stands apart
from the body. Moves always towards reset.
Never meets its rough and flinching twin."

BAT BRIDGE (. . . [BEGAT BIRD])

Our first folly lay in the breaching: doozy of a morning
where limb from jerky limb unfurled. See spright sprites
tangled up, grappling ceiling—a bat is just an upside-down
bird. I said *I'm going for a run now*, and daylight oozed
slow and yolky into Austin. Into that greenhouse of a room.
A run as rearrangement of the limbs to escape constraint.
By extension: we are running all the time. Which is not
to say, exactly, that the day was a wasted sequence
inside a sequence, malformed cells in division. Rather:
garbled transmission. Fruit before and after dicing.
I bent you these words to fit them under the bridge.
An escape hatch always overhead. If the hand extends
it extends for you. An egg is a locked room, too.

BAT BRIDGE (SELF-PORTRAIT AS SELF-PORTRAIT IN A CONVEX MIRROR)

In a city neither Rome or New York I throw
my clippings out. Beyond my glass lies swelter,

lichens, curved rim of the world sneaking up
from beneath horizon. John, reading you

is like peeking into a glory-hole, tracking
the contour of what emerges. Waking

to find familiar topiary shaved into strange
erotic shapes. I picture you, agog,

finding new and vexing reasons to write
of some dewy face from Parma, your hand

thrust mutely toward his own. Enacting,
with each clause, barriers against the urge

to reach across that upturned surface
and disturb the smoothness of his chin.

Beneath all that cloud-stepping comes
this exegesis of want. Forgive me

for my fluttering—the theses are many
and we have so little time. Just enough

to poke my finger against that stretched
canvas, feeling it twist about my point.

I've dallied in the funhouse for far too long.
Each sticky surface becomes transmission

or transcription—is light careening between
two mirrors. Encountering you, I extend

my arms: their wingspan scrapes the edge
of our enclosure, the width of a world.

LISABELLE TAY

MANGOSTEEN SEASON

After Philodemus the Epicurean, trans. Sherod Santos

It's the season of small-seeded mangosteens,
the season of lychees and orange-fleshed fruits,
of custard apples, of pungent nangka larger
and heavier than ostrich eggs, hiding sweet petals
from ripening, from consumption. Even so,
have you noticed how this year nothing's changed?
How the boats circle, island to island, weighted
with freshly shaven boys posturing, some trying
not to cry, necks craning toward the next
two years of national service, some to die?
How their mothers do not yet know this, how they
are packing their sons' leftovers carefully,
in old tupperware, with all the weight of love?

JOHN AT THE END OF HIS DAYS

grips a pen with crabbed hands   gazes bewildered
at crabs hunched along a shore   thinks to himself
Maybe you've got it wrong
It's not so strange that you fell at his feet
as though dead   he whom you loved   the firstborn
of the dead   Grief after all is a kind of failure
exile unending grief   Who are you to offer
comfort?   You are drowning
and survive via transmutation   memory into
mystery and all your days swallowed
by a bitter tongue   Your throat blazing
like the sun of his face swallowed now by snow
The white stone of your body worn smooth
with age   translucent by isolation
through which all that is hidden will be revealed
With each revelation your head sheds its hair   your skin covered
with old-person down   like the hairs of winter fruit
shaken free by a gale   Who is to say whether an angel
is embodied longing at the end of all knowledge
Who is to say   if your enemies are this moment rejoicing
over open tombs left behind   the mouth of the earth
your last recourse   Now you are weeping and nourished
for a time   and times   and half a time   by the thought
of a final bloody justice   a sickle swung reaping across
the dying earth and the return of a city with walls
Now his face is before you beloved   his words dry in your mouth:
Behold   *the sea is like glass*   *Therefore repent*

SOLARIUM

In his dream   the boy slips past blue iguanas coiled
glittering near a cenote's open mouth
plunges into watery prehistoric dark

    in his country there is little deepness
but yesterday—for the boy time is *now*
and *yesterday*—his grandmother drove
him down the east coast parkway flushed
with salt-leavened bougainvillea to the
airport: and he saw for the first time

    a forest breathing over falling water

His mother   presses a palm to curved glass, behind
which swift water free-falls into a basement
pool, cascade muted by an acrylic funnel

    reaches down to wipe the boy's open mouth
taps his chin as a reminder as if they were
in church, strangely solemn under the roof's
sloped oculus where rain gathers and spills
helpless to withstand its own power. The boy
is radiant, remote. Even silence is a kind of

    prayer, his mother thinks. Even falling

Her mother   has eyes on the waterfall. She considers
lymph, draining through the interstices
of her body and pooling, draining again

    rushing and returning like ocean milk
making its secret way through the clefts
between cells. Inching through myriad
channels unseen with each pulse of her heart
which has failed before. These days
she is creeping into herself like a turtle,

    furling budded into what is to come

ON THE CURATIVE PROPERTIES OF INCENSE

I am waiting as they stream out the gate
lidless and ashen, one by one—
without flowers in their matted hair falling
lank over white robes—
without recourse except the distant red
light blooming through my windows.

I have the pears ready, gold and succulent—
three soft mounds of rice, the huat kueh
and defridged oranges beading water.

The incense flaking in my hands.

There is no one to do it for me
so I peer through dimness into the mirror—
glass undulating in candlelight—
sweep the money over my body.

My fingertips lustrous with ground kunyit.
My eyes watering as if from a whipping.

They come with open mouths into the darkness
of my room, fall upon the food without care
or memory. My thumb finds the matchstick
in my pocket, pushes it down a length of
sand, phosphorus, powdered glass—
the resulting flame a thing of beauty.

Their feet leave no prints in the dust
as the incense curls through their scrabbling
hands. They, like me, are hungry
I, like them, am restless

PILGRIM

Last night I dreamed of a garden on the moon,

a stone rolled away, an empty tomb

a wall of violets dripping milk,

a harvest of joy

Today I will pack my bags and start walking

pregnant Lazarus freshly woken

collecting dew in living gourds

bread falling from the sky

I will kiss my husband before I go

dust sleep from his clean-shaven face

then leave slippery as an egg

PSALM OF PREY

    According to chrysanthemums.

LORD—
    through this murmur-winged
                          skirmish
I see the curve   of Your grey arm
   hewn
                 and dripping like   the end
  of an alder branch cut   in spring
in spring that You made   with all the faculties
             of God

        Surrel

SPIRIT—
    Pucks, mannikins   snapdragons:
all my enemies are here
          to enact violence
   on desire   in the flesh   of my body
content to break their teeth   elsewhere
        Can You see me?
                    Can You hear
the region kites circling
        round this body of flesh
   from whom thought   has parted

        Surrel

BROTHER—
      like a man in a parable
            I have forgotten   to walk
Your name in my mouth   unspent
    I must relearn the cast   of your broken limbs
          rearrange my own   likewise
Must remember   the dim breadth   of the world
     Your familiar legs striding   down the lane
          fingers dripping
                from the honeycomb

      Surrel

FATHER—
          I am crawling home
               animal come alive
  to the scent of its master's hand

      Surrel

THREE STARS

The smooth arc of a steel rule flicked over twice-ironed linen, white
      as forgetting. The pale shell undersides of fingers pressing

on a glass-foot, pulling it millimetres towards coherence.
      Such small beauties bloom behind my eyes as you educate me

on mise en place inside this heated dome, which seems to me a
      cloche and we the limp sprout soon to moulder. Around us dogwood

is bristling. I thrill briefly at the setting—cold, besotted
      precision—which after a moment diminishes. We, too, I feel

are likewise diminished. My thighs tighten at the deferential
      sweep of crisp napkin over my lap. My tongue dry as old bark.

               ***

There was a chef, you say, bright star of his generation. He
      killed himself. He had not yet lost a star; he simply felt it

inevitable. In the bathroom someone slips me a warmed
      towel, averting his eyes. It is right that he pretends no one

is crying over the sink. He is simply doing his job.
      Now I place a quatrefoil wafer on my tongue, reap

the curdled fruit of my own fear; espuma is dissolving
      into the table's unseen roots. A candle is brought over

to our table, burning between us as something else once did.
      Dark. Outside the black-bone trees draw water from the tired earth.

SELF-PORTRAIT AS A MOIROLOGIST

Rescuing you—not from death but
from oblivion—is perhaps a task at
which I will not fail. I will trespass
under the earth in silence, locate
your echo within my body. I will not
look back. Our childhood a talisman
between my fingers. Once we slithered
into a dry canal between a church
and a coffee shop. Once we rode
creaking swings all night without
speaking. We held hands in a chapel
like siblings in a forest at the mercy of
a witch. If I am honest I don't want a
new heaven, a new earth, new anything,
only the flattening silence of growing grass.
Under my feet your bones are waiting.
Under our feet warriors are racing their
horses to the ends of jewelled halls.
All day I gesture towards an alliance
with happiness. When I eat I think of
the unwholesomeness of seedless things.
The dangers of invention and many-
tongued memory. The beauty of a rigid
vigil under strips of white armour.
I suppose regret is the cost of living,
especially the sort that happens after
what you loved is gone. I will not speak
for you but to you. I will keep the soundless
wound of tenderness open. In this way
I can save you over and over again.

NATHANIEL CHEW

LANGUAGE ACQUISITION

once I filled a body, named it
the earth after some sown
home, departed for wilder
plots—first words
plucked from loamy wholes
for every flowering part, petal
by petal a blooming
holesomeness spelled out
of nothing, puddled holy
water at the boiling point
of blood perennial, unwelling
ink. to wright the world
as scripture is to upturn
loose soil until scree
returns sentences, rows
of lines running on, to scry
what roots take. nothing grows
without violence of a kind
handgrafted, lancing one landscape
from another, willing weather
odder to the touch, older than testament
otherwise. once I filled a body
with the year's four corners, spilling
shape like rivers runoff
the bold edge of each page
reread, watermarks singing
floods at every turn. this season
amnesic and its only remembered
sacrament on repeat—baptism,
baptism, baptism, naming
every green thing for some home,
some hymn the mouth mouths.

SET FOR A LITANY

EXT. THE INCONVENIENT COAST – IMPROBABLE HOUR – (wake up wake) – a MOTHER unfolds her IMAGINARY BICYCLE and screams off – salt morning lavering her REEF EARS – song like *summer wind carries us to places all our own* – MOTHER'S MOUTH like sock laugh – camera DOPPLERS – fishing POLES and fishing MEN bleed – into the same shape of LONGING – (so long so long) – lay their LIMBS along the BOARDWALKEDOVER SHORELINE – where the ALUMINIUM poles become RUST ISLANDS – the BAMBOO poles DRINK and DRINK and unfurl to SLURP the slowest CLOUDS – and plain old BONES well who knows – MOTHER dwells not on BONES – (fare well fare well) – tide out – CUT TO: – INT./EXT. THE COAST MOTHER'S HEAD THE COAST – THAT HOUR TWELVE YEARS THAT HOUR – drop anchor – IMAGINARY BICYCLE lurches – (bon voyage bon) – splinters now old growth BAMBOO SEAFOREST – (bone) – MOTHER sieving sand for a SPARE TIRE but won't look at her hands – (good) – she only has TWO but can't remember of what – (bone) – *ooooh seeing my tomorrows* – was the morning COMING or GOING – MOTHER WAVING or WAVE – (good) – (bone) – (good) – fingers blinkered busy – unfishing LINE after LINE

OOLOGIES: TWO AND A HALF PERSPECTIVES

I
can't break / a few eggs without / hands and a hard / place which could be / earth or other / holds other hands / the present day / families and living / rooms choke full / with lodgings / misfit to be fished / from gold spill / all dirt being / matter out of place / but what / if shell / shrapnel glued back / together like stained / glass and we / are the icons of / saints and we / are the inklings of / pulse and we / dream chalazal dreams / of suspension / bridges we've burned but can't / break

II
why
is an egg

timer
used for non

egg
circumstances are there

so
many emergences needing

alarum
in your palm

isn't
the rushed hour

aloud
enough in this

kitchen
jarring flour dust

bowls
from flatland frissoning

nutshells
in the unsaid

air
why do we

belt
all our wibbly

wobblies
with time and

shrill
song and when

will
our mouths remember

tasting
word before swallow

II.v
stately pleasure dome,
whirled, begotten, not made to
fall, over, easy,

LITANY FOR A PANTRY

Monday

Mother: Sandwich?
S: Sure I'd lov
Mother: Help yourself

Mother hands S a few ragged squares of cheesecloth, a butter knife, and long green beans, so long their ends trail over pans, toasters, microwaves, and over the edge of the counter, out of sight.

Mother: Butter's on the table
S: Oh sorry but wh
Mother: Oh that's right
Mother: You don't butter your sandwiches in your country
S: It's true we usual
Mother: I remember my college days the dumpy drainwater of one percent milk and not a single café had figured out how to make tea
Mother: Tea!
S: Good thing you left
Mother: Cheers

She holds up a piece of cheesecloth that has been origamied over and over itself into a sandwich, bits of bean peeking out.

Mother: Are you getting used to the local food?
S: Well I think
Mother: But I wouldn't blame you for having a sandwich every once in a while something simple for a change I mean look at me now
Mother: It's only when Dad isn't around that I get away with such debauchery he's a rice pot through and through
Mother: But something about the form of a sandwich is so satisfying you know it's like a jigsaw where you are the missing piece in the middle and chomp chomp chomp you unpuzzle ingredients like they were never born
S: I like to think of sandwiches as choose your own adventures
Mother: Same thing

Mother starts to butter S's cheesecloth.

Tuesday

S rummages through a flock of plastic bags on the floor. Each time she surfaces with a different gourd in hand and holds it up to her lips or nose or ear or chest.

S: Bitter gourd
S: Angle gourd
S: Bottle gourd
S: Ash gourd
Mother: Are you getting used to the local food?
S: I'm learning t
Mother: There's a trick to it
S: The names?
Mother: You take all the ones you don't like and pestle the mortar out of them until the skin colours run together and the texture is newborn and voila you've made something you hate even more than the slum of its parts
S: Oh but I like
Mother: Just add starch
Mother: Helps keep it down

Mother picks up a gourd with dreadlocks and takes a bite from it.

Wednesday

Mother: I'm going shopping
Mother: Are you getting used to the local food?
Mother: No rush
Mother: But I'm going shopping
S: What do you need?

Mother surveys her pantry in a panoramic swivel of limbs and longing.

Mother: Garlic bulbs
Mother: Light bulbs
Mother: A new nose for you
Mother: Just kidding they don't sell those
Mother: A new sense of humour
Mother: Also for you
Mother: Ever noticed how sense and sneeze have the same ingredients

Mother: But a sneeze makes you smile
S: Actually if you could pick up some oats for my breakfast that would
Mother: Bless you

Mother scribbles on her hand in pen.

Mother: Oat bulbs

Thursday

Mother: Are you getting used to the local food?
S: Actua
Mother: Grab a lime
S: Fresh or frozen?
Mother: I just need the shape

S opens the freezer, stares inside for a full minute.

S: I don't think we have any

Mother reaches both arms over S's head into the freezer. She lifts a whole, frozen, unplucked chicken up from its roost on the top shelf. Nestled underneath in wrinkled paper towels are three calamansi limes.

S: I
Mother: Unround
Mother: Unround
Mother: Unround enough

Mother closes the freezer and exits.

Chicken: I was working on the shape
S: I know
Chicken: Flavour is easy but shape takes time
Chicken: You can't mix shape can't potpourri a circle from three knobs
Chicken: And the temperature needs to be just right for moulding the molecules
Chicken: Which is hard when you're in a freezer
S: Can I help you?
Chicken: No

Chicken: All good now I'm room temp
Chicken: Just set me a timer will you
S: How long?
Chicken: Five years

Friday

S shimmies a handwritten note out from under a cartoon bird magnet on the fridge. She reads it. It's a short note.

S: Yes

She reads it again.

S: Yes
S: I am learning to throw my jaw to the wind
S: I am sleeping among the shelves between meals
S: I am filling with new home smell new home taste new home mouthfeel
S: I am brimming with getting

She reads it again, then folds it gracefully into her mouth, chews, chews, chews.

LANGUAGE REMISSION

sundown and body songs itself back to reflex angle ingrown cricket wing scrapes short to mid terms of memory to sandpaper air born smooth as babybreath rent riffled on angsana elbow knockkneed prefab gutter scarp scabs lossy with all that medium all turbulent betweens perhaps to score is also to score notching another call to caterwaul in minor key groove slashed grave overhead drag syllables out of silence out of sleepwalk which is easier pronounced still life tongue stopped traffic imagining itself travelled as tar or this bloodpurple please don't say blues yet hour of world leap year of leaving unheard and humming along anyway cell membrane solfege soma so many words to stitch false music drum up voice clear as crick dopplering back of throat cut chords loose lips from letterpressing for now let lung whisper lunged secret noise let breathbone vesper nothing sweet commas breveing let be let be

SCAR STORY

like any sunbleached souvenir
my scar tells so slant as to be
inscrutable. milk spill petal
pressed almond silver at my temple—
where is the story in that? where
is blood, for that matter, blanched
even in flashback from slick edge
of bathroom tile, speeding car, towel
grown heavy with all that wet life.
I young enough to scream and not
reverberate with the sound's leaving.
to feel needlepoint threading gash
and recognise neither
denouement nor grace. later unmade
stitches smooth today in my mirror's face
barely even seamed. this glimpse
of skin film in motion, fiche given
to tide. continental drift tugging me
from me, remapped by the minute. whole
oceans falling off the page. water unmuscling
a cupped memory of hands.

PATTERN RECOGNITION[1]

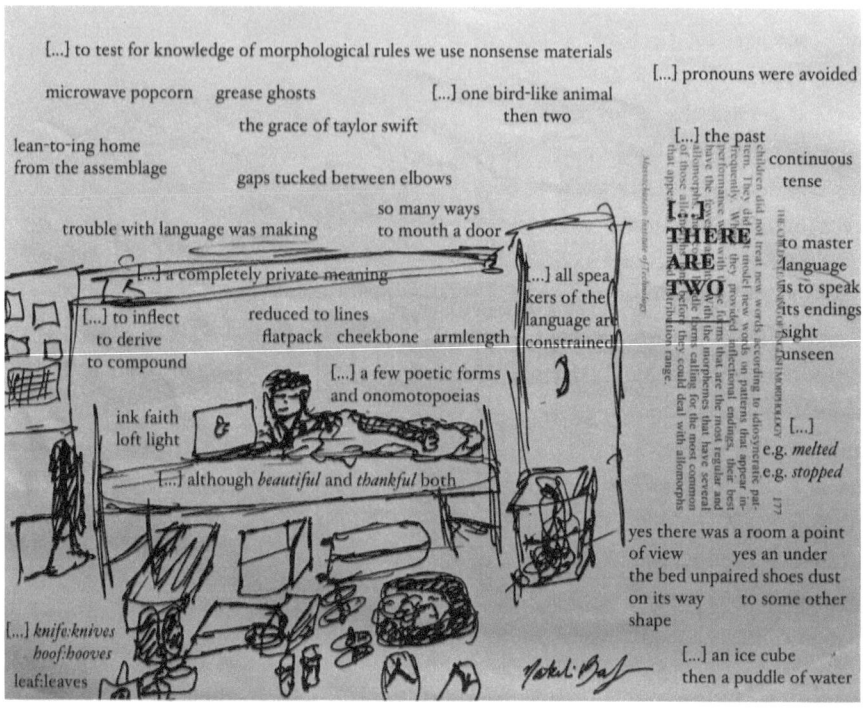

---

[1] Text prefaced with [. . .] is from Jean Berko, "The Child's Learning of English Morphology" (*WORD* 14:2-3, 1958).

Illustrations in black ink by Natalie B.

```
           song                    skying              roots
       of the holy          man    attending         almost
     cause enough         for    the word  whole    ashen bark
     somehow  the             whole rotting grafting height finds
     use  for shape         paperback blooms  monsooned mâché
     real lifelike   leftover    pinstripe scrap  pajama muslin outgrown
       home   out of inertia   cobbling wobbling something  more
        rubbled   tenants  dust known  parts  left  dreaming
         bulky  hemispheres of   cathode ray  televisions
            dolls  there  sun soured  raffia  halfhitching
           age into self sealing rings  flatpack nesting
            here a hold   for cardboard   boxing
              rust   at every  fork crook limb
              bend    or    memory shed
             to skin   straight as antennae
             crowns  where germ sprouted
             deck  topsoil  rutting   long
             need  pulsing  through void
             of newsprint  wire  scrap metal
              out  years ago   sepia seed
              like any tree     it grows ground
```

RAG   /   BONE[1]

---

[1] After Robert Zhao Renhui, *Singapore, very old tree*, no. 12.

AFTER ESCHATOLOGY

the prayer begins when there is no sin left
to the imagination. done to dust. you don't pretend
at made amends, that your clasped hands
will set the bones, myrrh the wounds, call the dead
to dinner. *penance* once meant *not enough*
and how do you uproot a hole like that? no,
the prayer is a song unspun to silk
on the tongue, blind stitch of sequence
and consequence, error and trial, aftermath
aftermath aftermath. there's nothing new to say
on both knees but the draw of borrowing
words was always the dark gravity of debt,
collection—of over tiding. the moon tugs
thirst to your surface. it is late
and the prayer is a metronome you try to make
lurch in reverse, substitute for the broken body
clock. it is late and you feel like jesus in his prime—
insomniac, sweating red, corpus for a hot minute
and by the weekend, atmosphere
in the tomb. in the space between hollow
and hallow, where your lips round to whisper
wet nothings, saltwater. the prayer is a fish escaped
from symbol, multiplying meaning
by zero, silvering your fingers in its wake. you blink
and lose the river. you wring your lungs
for weather. the universe shrinks to the present
tense. O heavens, O hells, O halfway
houses of half mirrors that O back,
just promise a landscape at the end
of the prayer, which truth be told is only a breath
held tight, carried into the wilderness beyond
amen—

LANGUAGE DEATH

  o   fill   me
    ear after   sow
   me de ar   wild
plot   fi st
upro t   who
    eve   et
      al   looming
     omeness   led out
           led holy
         oil   oint
              unwelling
     wri   t
   ripture   upt
o   unt
          o
        on to cry
          ing
   a kind
    raft   a   scape
 m   other illing   her
odd   old   amen
      I f   a body
  h ear s
h el   t e r vers o
   l edges   each
re d water   sin in
 d at e   seas
   s and   embered
    t o peat— is
  ism a   naming
ver g e thin or me me
  m y   mo th mouth

KENNETH
CONSTANCE LOE

EQUILIBRIUM FOR A HOT MINUTE;

a minutiae filter. a land of encouraging loss:
do manatees dream of kelp milk?
a year of feeling blindsided? some
days are lessons in how to shake
off the
sillage of snail
trails and agitation
in an attempt to keep restless,
reckless inertia
cavorting with a worrisome appetite
at bay.

would I have love-bombed you?

on *would*: some evenings start out
calm, relaxed in the kitchen, solitudinal
études, but a rumbling soon ensues,
muscular fatigue coupled with crepuscular
musings~Sitzfleisch goes missing,
and the body a deboned meniscus curving
unto the mind a velvet hibiscus.

recognise

thoughts need not trouble
the rubble rumble numbing a pointed
poignancy anointed pregnancy—another
journal nears the end but this one steeped
in significance boiling over bleeding buckets
of asphalt and apricot kernels and Fuji
apples and transitive
verbs and viable recipes for an implicit future.
words never failed thee, only reason rhyming
with the seasons and committing treason against
thy emotions. and a moment of
reckoning, of recognising that very

moment when you allowed yourself
a semblance of vulnerability, something
resembling sharing something vulnerable with a
resembled other, an ensemble of
confrontations, a mirrored lack.
fourths pickling into fifths, tickling
knees deep in on thin ice
impatiently awaiting another payout
this lockdown an étude in
longitudinal solitude

AN EMBARRASSMENT TO EMBALM

i.

Unravel from a single dent. something is unhinged, some
things are spoken and you imagine them as
salt crystallising on unsung wounds, searing
maroon into soft, off-pink, off you go chewing
more than you can bite, embarrassed to eat
lao hong sound bites, stale from proclamations
gone done you in, flux out, flex off, flummox.

ii.

The comma enjoys peering its
curled toes across sidewalks and wide boulevards
that every city that's ever been called the
Paris of the [insert geographical markers]
takes for granted and a lot of the
commas you see scurrying along said boulevards
seem out of breath and pressed for time
for every pause is an exhalation that empties
the tongue of its tip and an expiration
involves mould and potential diarrhoea
that excretes and excretes and excretes
as it syncretises all punctuation
with a predilection for pointes.

STRANGELY COMEUPPANCE,

you come upon a pot
of some skelter sans coat. And
six summers on, you know better
than to wish upon buckets
that would take you to another tree,
pine cones littered across snow-ridden
encounters down by the river—
you were chasing spiders across parch-
ment paper, whose stony webs left you
dangling in piles of angostura bitters,
inhaling deeply eau d'acceptance,
and you think to yourself:
Maybe this time, you are wiser,
You have looked into the mirror
And identified in the past year some
Traits of yours that you'd like to keep
Observing, in the stillness, when in motion,
In the company of others &
when alone.

ALASKA

Closing this chapter is more like a giant
trash container always in different states
of undress, sheathed in a thick gloss
that suffocates while preserving them roots in
a state of irrevocable rot. You cannot
smell the stench that bubbles just
beneath the impenetrable layer,
this glossolalia of abominable scents.
Instead visual enters your nostrils, shoving
its ways up like corona test swabs and massaging
hysterically the frontal lobes of your olfactory glands.

IT STARTS WITH A NIP,
a faint crumple of anticipation—pinch, squeeze,
unroll—or it doesn't, and the scene skips to the meat, already
sheathed, already ready, circling a ring, tantalising . . .
3000 BC: Pasiphae fending off King Minos of Crete's "scorpions and
serpents" with a goat's bladder. Intestines were an early favourite.
Imagine this slippery piece of paper that you're holding is Japanese
tortoiseshell, Egyptian linen, Chinese silk.
AD 2021: "You can't roll a condom onto a flaccid cock."[1] Trojan™,
Whirlpool, Stallion. bb, do you scroll hard and fast to the money shot
or let your excitement ebb and flow in agony as the reservoir of lust
floods every time a hole gapes? Luscious lips, Skyn on skin, blue
thumbs, fingers glide, limbs painting libidinal landscapes as I linger
on my orifice—*toccami*—they're sucking on the couch while I sniff
my pits, insert something, rub tenderly, bite bicep, lick something
thick as they ride each other into the horizon and my gaze licks the
screen, melts into it, and I forget to breathe. "Rather than being lovers
in order to breathe, we are queer in order to escape asphyxia."[2]
RealFeel, Unlimited Intimacy—protect, delimit—the fantasy is only
as real as what cannot be adequately represented (reverse money
shot?)—still, aroused, it rises—Fetherlite, not fertilise—presence of
latex starts to grate—"Condom To Bareback Gay Porn Videos
Showing 1-20 of 747"—take it off, keep it on, does it matter?
silicone is to water is to oil as illusion is to delusion is to perversion
keep those hips gyrating, they're churning that butter, tango till I
climax, in time, in tandem, sometimes to an earlier scene, where their
gaze meets mine—flaccid, I wipe my belly—a browser history of
shame precedes me, one that every jerk was an affront to, a body
that's used to disowning its desires, a body whose -ody still keeps
score but unwinds with every drip of hot wax:
"All I hear is moans, all I hear is groans /
 Out here on my own, I'm a semi-precious stone."[3]

---

[1] Paul B. Preciado, *Testo Junkie: Sex, Drugs, and Biopolitics in the Pharmacopornographic Era*
[2] Guy Hocquenghem, *The Screwball Asses*
[3] Zebra Katz, Shygirl, *LICK IT N SPLIT*

HOW MANY POTENTIAL BEAUX DOES IT TAKE TO CHANGE A FENNEL BULB?

this bulb is fused with salsiccia masquerading
as heteroflexibility obliviously waiting
in the wings of an overfamiliar embrace;
but how do I measure the warmth of an other
when there are a million and one reasons
why hot and cold are but two climes,
and love is neither deciduous nor evergreen?
so why don't you come up some time and slice me
nice on the bias of this precipice
where I don't care if it's affection or romance
any more than I care a lot
and the only thing complicated is vegetables—
a deconstructed salad on all fours
with three closets staring at your fronds?

NOT A NUMBER

that exacerbates but tangential desires
bubbling in the background
foregrounded by these pangs,
a cloak-and-dagger attention span
nipping the foreskin of my heart.

starboard decks deal a constant,
nagging unsettling veering
from their own bets—comets
wavering as they come
closer into my orbit (or I into theirs)
and somehow gravity seems so
much more malleable now than
2009 when my head
was an apple riddled
with wormholes and my ego
locked in a crypt up seven flights
of fancy near a plum sea
where waves loiter, refusing to leave,
and fragility was a word
you'd used to describe
boiled asparagus
on a bed of economic bee hoon.

YOU CAN ONLY BREAK A STEM WITH YOUR BARE HANDS IF IT'S DRY

and my heart is still moist from the melting slush
of first snow, still throbbing
from you ebbing away between my sobbing,
still pulsating from when you held the lips
of my fingers in the nook of my lower back.
a brazen warmth emanates from my nape—
I hope you know how much you inspire me
and with every expiration snipes a date that swipes me off
my right—senses reverberate.

I revel in the thought of thriving in parallel,
a Delphic gulf between us,
which my Sun in Libra insists on bisecting
with coin-operated binoculars but neither of us
has any spare change, and looking two illicit minutes
into the future is like traipsing into a cauldron,
Lilith's fortune cookie translated into three illiterate
crumbs—
just enough to confound and leave one pondering
but not enough to outwit the brew.

THERE IS A CHAIN THAT LIES BEYOND DAISIES

that engulfs expectations; a constant anxiety that plagues
the mother, the kindergarten teacher, the monarch butterfly—
they all crave the children getting along, caterpillars in May
clamouring for spring herbs and social approval.
Mother is high on dandelions,
cradling cocoons in her sundress,
one for each day of the week mirroring
the bunions on her wings from tying
cables, each cable a chore that she bore,
she a tireless pollinator,
Rose Quartz & Serenity,
tiring till the doldrums,
the doldrums: wings torn, cane sugar, cowering child.

LAEKEN PLACID

A crocodile *lays* on a bed of crocus with gently smiling jaws,
tanning its hide against walls festooned with smilax,
pondering the day Ms Birkin goes free-range.
The lake is caked with a sheath of moss green precipitate
insoluble in excess $C_{21}H_{27}C_1N_2O_2$.
A squadron of ducks bumbles along, the algae their canvas
as they brush their webbed feet with panache,
oblivious to the reptile's desire for kaeng phet pet yang
bubbling up in the broth of its belly.

vile bile of the Nile / let my body go / my body lies over the ocean /
my body lies over the sea / "the sea is History" —Derek Walcott

my body sends microwaves down his spine,
circling each intervertebral disc,
etching hickeys at every corner, every turn
belying the blood bath of Salzb-urgh. castle to castle,
lust to rust, caught in a landslide of arrogant cherubs
and Penelope in an infinity loop with no room to dust,
just pictures of Jap curry in cyanosis.

"I'm going to have to have an operation for tendonitis in the shoulder."   —Jane Birkin

sticks and stones may break my bones, but snakes and slugs
deify me. they tell me there is much tension around
my temples, "structural weaknesses" as the
Federal Buildings Agency would say.
i call upon my sister for mercy,
mercy for the slugs whose mucous talismans
callously adorn the steps of my altar,
mercy for the snakes who, after swallowing
fortune cookies in whole, spit out illegible bits
of waxen tender at my avatar, a 90-something-year-old
Nyonya grandma with more than a wishbone to pick.

"old womanly fatigue – a female centenarian"   —Bruno Maddox

what was the measure of a man?
was it the way one wore their cufflinks that peeked showily
through the stiff peaks of a double-breasted blazer?
the way culottes rested neatly on the hip, highlighting CK
waistbands and abdominal Vs?
or History, as told through the swampy annals of anal canals?
you might be surprised to learn that said canals plundered
the Silk Road and were Wunderkammern of chinoiserie,
all forbiddenly stitched on camels' humps, wakame and
bamboo plastered on tofu skin and wok-fried porcelain.

sugar spice and everything but rice—
a Range Rover guzzles La Chouffe in the indices of park
meets regulation on Avenue van Praet. it meets a young
British family right outside the Japanese Tower and they're
noticeably excited because it's their first time going to Japan!
when they get home, they're gonna watch Mulan because "it
kinda ties in to the Japanese Garden right?"

illicit vapours of coriander and sesame creep in
from the heavens. hell, already frozen, heaves
a roasting sigh at this little heathen, the love child
of acridine and a yuzu tree. Here, hear, a public service
announcement from a Parisian: uni should be consumed
alongside all other starchy foods such as baguettes,
crackers, etc. but "stop it with your rice."
sure, let's fuck up traditions and recipes and go wild with
ingredients, seasoning, sun, sea, sex (fuck university)—
well, I guess bánh mì wouldn't exist if the colonised didn't
get inventive and where would we be without bánh mì?

PITAHAYA IN THREE PARTS

A bag of groceries sleeps on the floor, carrot tops languishing beneath the weight of jars of raspberry jam, dishwashing liquid and cantucci. Eight metres away, a White Mustang is parked under a dragon fruit tree. Against the purplish 7pm sky, its paint glistens, coruscating pinks and whites interlaced with spotted shadows, as though the car itself was a giant dragon fruit sliced in half, exposing its juicy flesh and crunchy seeds in full glory. The mirage of this draws you in. You try to look away, but your field of vision ripples in defiance. You're entranced. Convinced that this is just a dream, you drop your phone without bothering to take a photo. You approach the Mustang like a comet pulled from orbit. 6 metres . . . 5 . . . 4 . . . You shiver in antici . . .

pation before sidling up to the chimeric car/fruit. "Can I take a bite?" "Sure. Might I recommend the headlights? They are a delicacy." "Well, I'm not sure I'd be able to stomach them. How about steeping them as tea? Would they still taste as good?" "Hmm . . . I haven't heard of anyone doing that before. It's worth a shot! I'll boil some water with my engine." [Motor whirrs as Mustang makes tea] "Here you go. I also decided to add some dragon fruit flowers that dried out on my roof." [Sipping] "Oh. WOW." "How is it?" "I've never tasted anything quite like this. Tarty . . . Oily . . . There's a mild bitterness to it that accompanies whiffs of alloys, followed by a floral finish. I imagine it would make quite an alluring perfume actually." "I think we're on

to something here." The bag rustles in the breeze. You turn around and realise the sky's already dark. The streetlights are on—they cast a halogenic pallor on the Mustang. You walk towards the groceries, slightly unnerved that the conversation was cut short. Can't there be something else you could hold on to? Instead of the bag whose contents you had already forgotten while in the self-checkout line. You remind yourself that carrot tops make a good pesto and everything else you had bought had a purpose—you just had to put it in context. Of what you're not quite sure, but you'll buy a dragon fruit the next time you see one, even if it was eighteen euros a kilogram. Then you remember that you could just pluck a ripe one from the tree, and so you do.

JACK XI

THIS SOLIDITY, OF COURSE, IS WHAT HUMANKIND YEARNS FOR

It's midnight, and the cement mixers
are still turning. It's always midnight
somewhere, do you ever think of that?
Always the coral fizz worrying the coastlines,
clock faces and poses suspended in stone.

A lone woman draws fewer shrimp in her nets;
new seawalls and jetties soak in hot silence.
There's always vans frotting a stippled ramp.
There's always a building with its lights on,
boiling. Always a pit
        for the bubbling block grey.

A cement mixer has a mud drum of grit
with a corkscrew to stir it,
        a chute to spill liquid
        and a driver to cry.

Turn over in bed now,
somebody is swimming. Floodlights
are testing tough skin through the rain.
Echoes relent across the ribs
of the complex: rough spatters of heaving,
caked hands on the drain. Lit from below,
he clambers pallid, hair tamped.

A trundle of glops
    and a humming drum spinning;
        the swimmer relaxes.
It's time for the bath.

(Endnote: Title from J. Watts' article "Concrete: the most destructive material on Earth.")

A SEASON OF SLIME

Walking through the early pandemic
I saw snails. Clustered under the lids
of circuit boxes and bins,
or painting plain walls. Then the slugs
in school, dried into curls or
stepped on.

Through the early pandemic, blame: bat blood
spread across a city's chopping boards.
Ash paste smeared on all palms
and instructions to wail.
As if everyone drove oil rigs into lush mud.
As if everyone makes trunks seep with both hands.
As if the workers who droop behind counters.
As if those locked in dorms and pushed into trucks.

In the early pandemic, I watched a video showing
how to completely cover your hands in black paint.
Of course it symbolised soap, but I couldn't see past it.
Black ooze from dispenser nozzles. Black handprints
on my pants, mask noses, lift buttons.
Lumps trickling down the dark back of my throat.

I don't think people are a virus.
I do think some of us are snotworms.
Snotworms live in the bones of dead whales.
Glue to the corpse they can't live outside of.
Dribbling out acid to melt and thus *eat*.
Growing grand off what falls from the nose of the dollar.

In some myths the world begins as slime:
a slurry of mud, divine sneezes or cum.
Stretched between a god's fingers and shaped into crystal.
I'd give anything to be held between a man's hands,
kneaded, awakening, fresh prints in my skin.

So much life starts in slime: amoebas, people,
salp colonies with phlegm nets, fresh balls of new slugs.
So much slime from inside eggs,
between bodies and joints.

I will stand with my dredged legs, my columns of snot.
We can rise ever dripping, ever gathering our muck.
Touch our palms to the dream, and then handle that clear gel.
To some new pull and toughening,
some faceting flash.

(Endnote: Partially inspired by Craig Santos Perez's "New Year's Eve and Day in the Chthulucene"; Lee Ann and Shona's "slimy sterilisation"; Alex Rogers' "The Deep.")

LA MALEKZORCISMO DE LA KVIRA KORPO

(the anti-exorcism of the queer body)

I. THE HOLY GHOST
came upon me like a blanket of lead.
Two colonisations gave us thick sheets of ghosts.
They swear I will not be charged so I trail my lips
    down another man's neck.
This islandwide silence foreshadows the sky.
That cloud on the horizon will not bring rain.
There is an inevitability to a crowd.
Bacchus was killed by the strong mobs of Jesus,
    stolen Bacchus who wined from another man's mouth.
Look: Jesus also died because of a crowd.

II. I AM
swallowing their words before them the same way I did
their theodicy. I have swallowed many things that had legs
that kicked and bulging eyes. There are things that
could have been universal, a language that they could have
known. I keep my teeth still as truth babbles in my gut like
the jumping chunks of a plague Egyptian. I am waved aside.
When I topple into the stall to vomit my frogs
there are no two men to flank my exit, no angel
to squat by my door. Well, thank fuck
    I still got a Judas.

III. GOD
fizzed in my insides like bacterial fission, papered over
my mouth with a thick film of cells. When I tongued free I
watched Him root in the napes of my parents, their arms
fruiting branches of hot ash and gas. I blinked and they
grinned. Wombless I rolled the cold eye of the ultrasound
over my belly, saw twenty clear foetuses budding like
grapes—this is number six and I am in the corner heaving
 , jaw smarting   , they watch the jelly tailed in umbilicus
the wet thing smiling all over they hug it to pulp and i
       feel more gel climb up my throat like a sentence
                  like prayer   like love

THE FEELINGS OF OLD WOMAN LEE

The ball slides through its slot
      with a bright yellow knock.
She pores until someone else says
      look, it's right there.
I'm not sure how to ask
      if she's uncomfortable with help.
I draw eyeballs on my bingo sheet.
She tells me she's afraid of snakes
      and other wriggling things.
If she sees one it slithers
      through her head at night,
      wakes her screaming.
So I draw a dog.
I ask what she used to do.
She says she made buildings.
She says she used to *bǎng tiě*
      stumbles over the word like
      it's a loose ingot *maybe it's*
      the wrong word she says
      but I see years of her
      knotting brown rebar
      together with string,
      swaying small and
      harnessed
      in the high-rise wind—
She laughs and says I'm just
      too young to know the pain.
She stuffs the bingo prizes in her bag
      like they matter.
She asks how long I'll be in the army
      and how much it hurts.
I realise at this point I know enough
      Chinese to ask about
      her biggest regret.

Her hands are old like wax or burnt
        coral, ridged against the light.
Marker ink on her fingers
        like silly green scars.
A gold ring on each hand and the stiff
        kind of silence.
I draw a soldier's cap on the dog, say
        look,
            bīng gǒu!

(Endnote: 兵 (bīng) as in soldier, 狗 (gǒu) as in dog.)

IN THE GUTS OF YOUR MOONCAKE AN EGG

Four frames and a watcher after Bae Young-Whan's
"Abstract Verb - Can you remember?"

My sister points, silent. Beyond bends a neighbour, stock-still before lock: in her hands is damp toilet paper. Beak peeping and squirming slick pink. My lips purse. A mynah.

Thank you, Linda. Now, we're talking PESTS. You know that they're cunning. A REAL PROBLEM. So throw out your spiced gel your wet rice your green meat. Serve mynahs.

Singapore is an inked little booklet of birds. Import-chiffon flamingo. Underdressed pigeon. Fine ibis, wild chicken, sharp brahminy kite. At the top of that tree is Sir Mynah.

A traffic warden swatting the wind's wet leaves. Limbs go ambiguous as he shoulders his coat: damp orange rustling, wolfish look clearing hood. He has spotted the mynah.

My mother stops. "*That's* what they're eating now?" She twists crisp chicken limbs free. "Isn't it *awful,* Jack?" I nod, mouthing meat. Outside our window, a chuckle—

A LOT LIKE OURSELVES

With thanks to Andrew Kirkrose Devadason

Text sourced from the Business Insider Nederland *article titled:*
"We visited a meat-processing factory
to find out exactly how McDonald's hamburgers are made"

i. nothing is allowed to go loose in the factory

jewellery and small pieces of bone must be removed
    jewellery and small pieces of bone must be removed
        jewellery and small pieces of bone must be removed
            jewellery and small pieces of bone must be removed
                jewellery and small pieces of bone must be removed
                    jewellery and small pieces of bone must be removed
                        jewellery and small pieces of bone must be removed
                            jewellery and small pieces of bone must be removed
                                jewellery and small pieces of bone must be removed
                                    jewellery and small pieces of bone must be removed
jewellery and small pieces of bone must be removed
    jewellery and small pieces of bone must be removed
        jewellery and small pieces of bone must be removed
            jewellery and small pieces of bone must be removed
                jewellery and small pieces of bone must be removed
                    jewellery and small pieces of bone must be removed
                        jewellery and small pieces of bone must be removed
                            jewellery and small pieces of bone must be removed
                                jewellery and small pieces of bone must be removed
                                    jewellery and small pieces of bone must be removed

    jewellery and small pieces of bone must be removed
        jewellery and small pieces of bone must be removed
            jewellery and small pieces of bone must be removed
                jewellery and small pieces of bone must be removed
                    jewellery and small pieces of bone must be removed
                        jewellery and small pieces of bone must be removed
                            jewellery and small pieces of bone must be removed
                                jewellery and small pieces of bone must be removed
                                  jewellery and small pieces of bone must be removed
                                      jewellery and small pieces of bone must be removed
jewellery and small pieces of bone must be removed
    jewellery and small pieces of bone must be removed
        jewellery and small pieces of bone must be removed
            jewellery and small pieces of bone must be removed
                jewellery and small pieces of bone must be removed
                    jewellery and small pieces of bone must be removed
                        jewellery and small pieces of bone must be removed
                            jewellery and small pieces of bone must be removed
                                jewellery and small pieces of bone must be removed
                                  jewellery and small pieces of bone must be removed
                                      jewellery and small pieces of bone must be removed

ii. per shift

dozens of people are on time
registered at birth
routinely brought to the meat

they go through the metal detector
they wash their hands in the cold
they separate containers
holding a mix of fresh and frozen shapes
    they turn between machines, ice, and mince
employees check other employees

water vapor keeps the production going

trucks collect time,
    turn in their lots
boxes disappear

the reception processes 45 to 60 people within a shift
the reception area even smells like beef

before they leave
another sticker is placed on them
a numbered tab of colour
on an arm brow or back

fewer people go out than in

iii. creation myths

a hamburger is typical hunter-gatherer fare
    it took ranged gear like arrows
or boomerangs, pneumatic harpoons
true civilisation began with the advent
    of mass hamburger production

                      the surface of the earth was minced
                      meat
                          and then *He* came
                      brought a deep chthonic sizzle
                          to the mantle
                      dipped a rod into the soft raw ribbing
                          split it into shapes
                      each patty a continent
                      each grease patch a sea
                      man and woman He created them sweaty
                      everything of one meat,
                          so very distinct

the life cycle of a McDonald's is as follows:
within a week of a cow's death
    a McDonald's is attracted
within two, there are seats and a counter
within three, there are faulty sauce dispensers
    they pop the pump open
    so you can scoop out the chili
BEHOLD, a rectangle
    of thick salty orange

                    the serpent dropped over an oily branch, said
                    the true fruit of the jungle has an interest rate
                    it lacks root networks with fungi and germs it lacks
                          four stomachs, tits, hooves, calves,
                                      and meat

first contact happened because of the burgers—
seems aliens love frozen liquidised egg
        and the matte texture of morning buns—
papers are written about space dumping grounds
companies jockey to eject their products
        further out, wrapped
      between slow-blinking stars

iv. some burgers are always tested

I was registered for birth in a McDonald's country
    every morning I wake up and
radio waves move through me
I am never more than a few kilometres away
    from the arches

                      a country is a business model
                          welfare a phase

        I have water,
      nutrients, time, and warmth
I have an apron and a barely slanted name tag   I wheel myself to work
                                                I wheel myself I wheel

                I am up to McDonald's standards
                work is a special kind of time
                work is the right kind of place for me

            I do not dream of cows

I blink and remove
lid from dispenser
finger from thumb   I do not   leave   my counter
crust from toilet   I do not   leave   my station
jewellery from meat   I do not   leave my   body
                          I do   not   leave   my body
                          I do   not
                          I do
                          I do   my body
                          I do   not
                          I do
                          I do   my body
                          I do
                          I   leave,
                          I   leave,
                           I   *leave!*
                            I
                             I
                              I
                               I
                                I

                                                 it can all be processed.

v. operations manual

1. we make sure cows are always slaughtered
2. we make sure the slaughter is incredibly fast
3. nothing is allowed to go loose in the factory
4. this space is filled to the brim with cold
5. this space is for all kinds of containers
6. a smaller surface area
    makes a quality employee
7. go through the metal detector
8. stand in a container
9. remove meat from the hook
10. contain the meat in a machine
    then activate it
11. when the minced meat looks like spaghetti
    it is perfect
12. find the exact cow the meat came from
13. put a new label on the box
14. ensure 75 hamburgers a second
15. put a new label on each box
16. nothing is allowed to go loose in the factory

vi. meat from five or six cows in one container

five or six cows
five or six cows
five or six cows
five or six cows
five or six cows

    five or six cows
    five or six cows
    five or six cows
    five or six cows
    five or six cows

        five or six cows
        five or six cows
        five or six cows
        five or six cows
        five or six cows

            five or six cows
            five or six cows
            five or six cows
            five or six cows
            five or six cows

five or six cows
five or six cows
five or six cows
five or six cows
five or six cows

    five or six cows
    five or six cows
    five or six cows
    five or six cows
    five or six cows
    five or six cows

        five or six cows
        five or six cows
        five or six cows
        five or six cows
        five or six cows

            five or six cows
            five or six cows
            five or six cows
            five or six cows
            five or six cows

                five or six cows
                five or six cows
                five or six cows
                five or six cows
                five or six cows

vii. worry seems to be growing exponentially

each representative wants nothing binding.
only risk, the entire chain of production,
to grow or spoil,
compiled with the pepper;
the world his burger.
nothing's limited-edition now.

they've found something:
sustainability. how serious!
they will make more bacteria vegetarian.
the world may be slightly different
because of the amount.

if there's something wrong,
they could easily turn over production.
they just need each country wrapped over in plastic.
fewer people in the mix.

viii. the microbes that cause rotting are a lot like ourselves

we live on cows
  we guarantee turnover
    we need water, nutrients, warmth and
      large surface area to volume ratios
        we can be produced within a few hours
        we are the organic results of code
          replicas
            textured and inexact
              time grills and tastes us
                we are limited-edition but we remain
                we can't decide on our own impact
                we are salt all over the world
                sometimes unnoticed
                we do not keep going
                we disappear
                we
                      are a chain
                        of similar complaints
                  a chain of unlikely
                concerns and questions
                motes made of metal, loose objects, and time
              we contact each other
            we are unlikely
          sometimes we are allowed to grow
        meat attracts us
      sometimes we are eaten
      sometimes we remain sometimes
    we remain sometimes
   we remain sometimes
we remain

THE MERMAN DYE AND ANOTHER MAN TALKING

A two-man conversation after Club Ate's "Dyesebel"

He uncouples smoothly and I see bone. Wet pelvis.
I have to turn away as he sets down the conch and the mirror.
He sings. I hear fish shoaling, a monsoon of fins, liquids kissing.
It's 3am on the steps of this river. I hear distant party laughter.
Behind us the buildings cut the night right open. As water swells
and chops the light into fluid rings, he speaks. Over the hush of his liquid
we talk about birds, about cities, why we'll never want children.
My shoes soak through. Eventually he says *you can look now*. I turn,
and he has a tail. His legs lie aside, trailing long organs

so many think accusation, smooth proof of our lies. I think of squid.
The lie is what they think that men need to have. *My mom watched that show,*
he tells me, and unclips his earrings. *I thought her name was "DYE-see-ble".*
I remember inking the dresses, until they let me use my brother's clothes.
Owning my lines. He's still wearing his binder; it shines, saltwater stains
bleeding through. He quips about what flesh he can't leave and I twist my lips.
The water still teems; the eels worship his tail, the dark fluid length
of his freedom. Heart breaking, I quip about worship. He grins, lifts the conch
and the mirror, cleaves the light to uncouple my hips. Our eyes meet. He sings, and

                                                                    liquids

                                                                    kiss.

THE PURPOSE OF FRUIT

You told me there was a fork in your past.
      I picture you distant, unclipping plastic
off all the babies, hand pressed to incubators
      like fevered foreheads: the lights switch,
and you're staring instead at rays
      splayed through microns of green. There are bulbs
swelling through the gel that you bless, bowing:
      an oath of steady wood, orchards devout
past drought. Instead we're in your car
      under the passing slant of the rays of roadside
green. After discussing punctured young guts,
      you ask if God told me to do plant science.
Surely my prayers bore fruit? No: black seeds
      in the guts of an ape, splayed out over
highway. Mom, I think of your papayas
      growing whole past our rooms: seeds repeating

pith in marred degrees. I see us
      by a cartoonish tree: a thick swollen jackfruit
with a house's girth, dark hidden acreages
      of flesh. My hand pressed to seedless skin
as its tree bends above us, a failed trebuchet.
      I say mildly, "I'll look it up later." You sigh,
waiting for the tree to snap back up.
      You are waiting for erupting seeds,
for flesh that gives under forks. You are waiting
      for fruit that is whole as Christ's nose
and a truth you suspect is in drought.
      I hunt through my stomach, gouge out dark
pearls, staring: meiosis mars pasts
      but I see your hand on my head through old fevers,
us chuckling over my uneven-cut melons.
      I wait for you to soften
and to say
      "Okay."

MOK ZINING

FLORISTRY BASICS: CUTTINGS

a word is a cutting,
   a sentence,
a bouquet.   when
   the inflorescence
wilts,
       scatter
            cuttings   in
a tub   of water.
   allow words
to float   as
they absorb   the new
   context
into which
   they have   been

   plunged.

FLORISTRY BASICS: SYNONYMS

each cutting is
unique, but that
is not   to say
despair   is
the only rational
response to
wilting.   Look
for a   synonym,
if   necessary, in
the catalogue.
there   they are
novel, updated
daily.

EXEMPLARY ARRANGEMENT C: "COLONIALISM: ADAPTIVE REUSE"

The following 1984 arrangement was presented by then Second Deputy Prime Minister Mr. S. Rajaratnam at a Seminar on "Adaptive Reuse: Integrating Traditional Areas into the Modern Urban Fabric".

When Raffles founded Singapore in 1819, it was the home of a few hundred fishing folk. All we know of its past prior to this are vague hints that it was used as a halting place by mariners, traders and pirates before they moved on to more congenial places. What happened before 1819—if anything worthwhile happened at all—has been irretrievably lost in the mists of time.

[. . .] Singapore's genealogical table, alas, ends as abruptly as it begins. However we could have contrived a more lengthy and eye-boggling lineage by tracing our ancestry back to the lands from which our forefathers emigrated—China, India, Sri Lanka, the Middle East and Indonesia.

The price we would have to pay for this more impressive genealogical table would be to turn Singapore into a bloodly battleground for endless racial and communal conflicts and interventionist politics by the more powerful and bigger nations from which Singaporeans had emigrated.

So from our point of view, to push a Singaporean's historic awareness beyond 1819 would have been a misuse of history; to plunge Singapore into the kind of genocidal madness that racial, communal and religious imperialism is today devastating so many underdeveloped and even developed countries. The present government, much to the dismay of local racial and cultural chauvinists, has been careful about the kind of awareness of the past it should inculcate in a multicultural society.

LESSON ON CUTTINGS: TRIMMING UNNECESSARY AFFIXES

Raffles to his Patroness Princess Charlotte, Duchess of Somerset,
—23 January 1823, Singapore

Since I last wrote to your Grace, about a month ago, I have had another very severe attack in my head, which nearly proved fatal, and the Doctors were for hurrying me on board ship for Europe without much ceremony. However, as I could not reconcile myself to become food for fishes, I preferred ascending the hill of Singapore, ███████████
██
██
████████████

                                                                    where, if my bones
must remain in the East, they would have the honour of mixing with the ashes of the
Malayan kings; and the result has been, that instead of dying, I have almost entirely
recovered.

EXEMPLARY ARRANGEMENT C: BACKGROUND & DISCUSSION QUESTIONS

Under British rule, Singapore flourished and attracted migrants from all over the region, becoming a uniquely multiracial community. While multiracialism is our strength, it is also our Achilles' heel and, as such, we must never take interracial harmony for granted.

Demonstrate how our unique brand of governance is designed to manage the dangers inherent to our diverse society. Explain how the arrangement of multiracialism equips us with the language to participate in intercultural dialogue and keeps the conversation within bounds.

[10 marks]

BESTSELLING BOUQUETS:
VANDA MISS JOAQUIM PENDANT

Thanks to its hybrid and multicultural origins, the *Vanda* Miss Joaquim is one of the most unique and beautiful orchids in the world. Like Singapore, it boasts a fiery core that culminates in resilience and an inner passion that radiates outwards into elegant shades of violet and rose.

Having plated free-flowering *Vanda* Miss Joaquims since 1981, we are unrivalled in both tradition and expertise. Hand-picked and preserved in full bloom, our *Vanda* Miss Joaquim pendant brings out its wearer's natural qualities of grace and refinement—the perfect gift for all occasions.

ORCHID BASICS: LIP MODIFICATION

In an orchid, labellum
formation is the product
of competition between two
protein complexes. To

mute trait,
infect orchid with
viral genomes

designed specifically
to silence

lip expression.

LAETITIA KEOK

GRIEF WORK

In your mother's tongue, the word for love
& the word for grief is only a difference of tone.

How easy it must be, to mistake one for the other,
sifting through memory for a lifeline to hold onto.

I want to ask: did you stay because you thought
you could knead sorrow tender?

Hand down your own throat until you could
say it right for him?

Here is how I know I am your daughter:
I, too, stayed, for the way

my name, rearranged, on a lover's tongue
made mercy of my mother's first creation.

But how to tell you, she is all the beautiful
you have wanted me to be, & all the cruel

I have wished for you? How to tell you
she loved me too & I knew then

I would mourn her forever?

Like you, I learn there is no difference
between who we leave & who leaves us,

only a soundless absence, wide as grief,
vast as love.

You would tell me to forget, but like you,
I want to remember my name.

Like you, I know: to forget is to die.

Once, I tried to imagine holding the girl: her body
draped over mine, the soft falter of her breath

ringing in my ears. For a while, we do not speak.
All around us, the world ends.

Then, she cradles me. She traces the break in my life
line, & tells me the story of my life.

This is what a body does: invent a memory to survive.

THE RIVERS OF US

We are in bed.
        I tell you stories:
My childhood

home was two storeys
        high, with bright
yellow cupboards &

stairs my sister &
        I liked to leap off
like frogs.

My mother kept
        a jar of saga seeds
in a locked drawer.

I know because
        she showed me.
Poured them into

my open palm &
        made me count: *nine*,
she said, *for eternity*.

I did not know, then,
        the word
for desire

would have the shadow
        of your name,
or the heat of your

body, trembling against
        mine. I have come
to know tenderness

is just another word
  for fear—for guilt,
for my mother's yearning,

which is now also mine.
  I imagine
she once loved a girl, too.

How else to explain
  the way the sky wept
when I was born

fingers curling around
  the throat of a desire
I could not yet name?

She was a girl once.
  She must have
known hunger,

must have weaved
  her body into
the body of a girl

& tasted a want so guttural,
  there was no end &
no beginning.

Yet I am proof that love
  does nothing.
It is not that easy,

I know—who, at the catch
  of a promise,
could choose death?

We are in bed.
  You ask me
for a better story. I say:

When I love you, I think
        the world will end,
red string ribboning

our skin to shreds.
        How can it not?
You laugh &

I think there must
        be a word for this,
but of course

there are no words at all.
        Only your body
weaving into mine,

entangling us.
        We are water.
So this is drowning.

On the shoreline
        of another river,
I watch a girl
touch my mother
        into existence.
Scooping thirst

from her lips,
        with her lips,
gathering guilt enough

to rename the universe.
        I hear her say,
come, let us be fish,

& they are water.
        They are inventing
beautiful things.

We are in bed. The girl
         touches me
holy. I touch her raw.

There is no language
         for this.
We are inventing one.

ETYMOLOGY OF MY MOTHER

       eldest girl: meaning least-loved—meaning any man
harsh enough to know that the human heart is the size of a fist

       bruising: walls—spine bent around forgiveness, skin
chafed into bone, tender mouths swallowing

       eggshells: grief, hanging from the clothesline, while you
are teaching me math, while I am carving

       this poem: from the rubble of photographs that will make
you cry—how do I look at you with the eyes he gave

       me: stomaching a December weary of exit? you will
always be the kind of ache that cuts like knife, the kind of

       beautiful: that betrays memory—like a birthmark, I
will always carry the debt of this life, as if nursing

       a wound: or suckling a child, I will always look
at the man you love, picturing flight—because I am

       your daughter: most-loved, less kind, pressing tongue
to ulcer, nail to blister, unspooling time, undoing you

       -r selfless: I will always beg you, with the hands you gave
me—haemorrhaging, deathless—to leave, to choose, to *please*

       choose better: I promise, in the quiet of the years where
you were neither wife nor mother, I was still the daughter who

       loved: you endless.

THE LOVERS BECOME BUTTERFLIES

But isn't that what love is?   To leave you a different person?

        To cleave memory from the knees of a lover,
        & still, remember otherwise? Tonguing her
        name into something you can bear, forgiving
        the impossibility of touch?

                Every person I have ever loved, I have asked
                them to stay. An ant scrambling from an anthill,
                two moths circling the edge of infinity. In the story
                my grandmother tells me,

    the butterfly lovers emerge from graves. To die
    for love, to die to live: the knife's edge of
    survival. In Mandarin, the word for love sounds
    like *I*—how selfish that

every girl I have ever loved, I have asked for
another lifetime. Cupped distance in hand &
begged for more. If love is anything, I am told,
it is to ask for more. Can I call this

        love, then? Tell me again, who I am. Show me,
        a vertex & its unbecoming. Bring my fingers to
        the flinch & split. Teach me, to die of thirst. How
        much I would give to carry

                a promise, unblinking, to shore. To die & die
                & die, across a terrain of desire. Let me tell you,
                my love, nothing has moved me more than
                your absence.

IN DEFENSE OF MY GRANDMOTHER'S BITTERGOURD SOUP

To prepare 苦瓜汤, my grandmother spoons away the gourd's insides, scraping seed the way one would hollow a body.

As a child, I would squat beside her, fanning the flame, watching yolk bleed into soup like a broken horizon.

I would watch the movement of her hands, scored with age, and she would tell me the first lesson she learnt as a girl:

吃苦, to bear pain—to eat it—the body a vessel for which grief passes through, staggers into.

Steam laps at my cheeks, and I close my eyes to a memory: my mother, pressing her lips to all my bruises,

mothering shrapnel into something beautiful. She says: *look, your skin is blooming,* and I open my eyes to

every body my grief has ever taken, running like rivers through me. The fold of his shirt, the earthquake

hands of a girl. But first, it was my mother's—nestled in her womb, delivering wreckage.

It is said that what you eat compensates for what you lack—have we not enough grief?

I touch myself and come away with blood. If you become what you eat, then, here: a stomach of hurt,

pooling like blades. The soup simmers. *Hold your breath,* I am told, *and you will not taste a thing,*

not the bodies washed ashore, not your body—a shore
of unforgetting: the translucence of memory

dripping off the kitchen table, into the gaps between the
kitchen tiles. Bringing the soup to my lips, my grandmother

tells me a secret: we are at once emptied by what we swallow
—I hold my breath, I swallow.

MAXWELL FOOD CENTRE (1997)

After Sharon Olds

you look at this woman in front of you &

you think you could not love her

more. she is beautiful. she could never be

more beautiful. you look at her & see

your entire life: four children, all beautiful,

the house we will cavity. let me tell you this.

she will only bear you two. you will only

love her for as long as you do not

have us. I will hate you for it. she will stay &

call it love, because she knows nothing else.

I will hate her for it.

my sister will be born hungry &

you will hate her for that—

hunger terrifies you. it is clear to me now.

if only, I think, *she had wanted more.*

I am sure you loved her once. you, now,

watching the woman who sits across you,

hair flaying the beauty mark on her right cheek,

is it memory that binds you?

the birthmark on her left calf,

her bellybutton before carnivore?

is it memory that betrays her? your hands

not yet switchblade, her knuckles not yet

bloated? what I would give to tell

all that I know now? my life, my sister,

my mother—

this woman in front of you—

I look like her, or she looks like me.

LAETITIA KEOK

she is beautiful. I am beautiful because of her.

                                                        she is so young. you are so young.

you think this is love, but it will not be.

                                                        will you believe me? in the years to come,

you will swallow love & spit it out different.

                                                        deboned & hollow, you will leave

only cartilage & fear.

                                                        trust me, I have lived it all.

I am here to give us all a chance.

                                                        here, under these moth-flecked shadows,

there are lives not yet lived:

                                                        I am not yet your daughter.

she is not yet your wife.

                                                        you still love her.

there is still time.

OBJECT PERMANENCE

We are back in the restaurant from years ago,
my grandfather choking on a fish bone.
I am too young to be afraid
but old enough to remember the sound of it:
not the staccato of his breaths, but my uncle screaming
blood, my aunt picturing shrapnel corkscrewing down
his oesophagus—fear nicking their throats clean.
The waitress tells him to swallow mouthfuls of rice
without chewing. I hold my breath & imagine
that is what dying feels like: the expiration of a heart—
a slow decay in which my father cannot meet his father's eyes.
I am old enough now to have seen it happen again,
to know we are always dying
little deaths: with my grandmother, with one half
of a body phantomed in grief, with the years after
absence. So much time & none at all. Things die
without dying. Things die & yet,
here: a husband, a son, the woman
they must have loved—leaving footprints in flour.
While my grandfather chokes, my cousin
stares out the window & pretends to be a fish,
whittling at the insides of her cheeks.
I watch her & tell myself a story in my head:
she is the half-eaten hong ban on the table in front of us.
When she was alive, she swam with other fish. Now,
open-mouthed & slit, marrow in my grandfather's throat,
she learns we are always fish, begging
for permission to leave.
On the way to his heart, the bone hesitates.
My grandfather stops choking. It is the cruellest
kindness. I watch my father hold his father in a death
grip so tender, I can almost hear him say: *all I want in this life*
is to love you permanent. All I want is to love you
permanent.

WORMS VIRK

20 AUGUST 2019, 9.03 P.M.

You can only forget things you used to know. It's the absence like a missing milk tooth that reminds me this is a devolution. Some people say you need to forget things to grow up. I guess in some ways you do – the brain is a sponge, not an ocean, and it will push certain things out so that you can learn how to file taxes and pay your insurance and shut up when someone else is talking. Someone else is talking, tongue licking the backs of their teeth, hard consonant sounds, this is the world I live in. This is the world we all twist upwards into, in embryonic denial.

You can only forget things you used to know.

I have forgotten how to love my mother. My mouth has gotten so big it takes me years before I run my tongue over the smooth gummy patch where we used to be. The tongue likes lacunae. The body likes sticking itself in places where other things used to be. Houses, jobs, other people's lives. I find my body attracted to this particular absence. We run our tongue over it a thousand times, counting the seconds that make up a day, another day, three hundred and sixty days of forgetting, forgotten, forgotted.

When I was a little bit younger, I put my tooth under a pillow so my mother would come back after she had finished tucking me in. I lose twenty teeth for her, but twenty times I fall asleep and my dreams are so loud I don't hear her in my waking world. Twenty mornings I wake up and put a coin that used to be a tooth into a piggy bank because my mother and I are saving for my university. We are paying for my education with teeth.

My mother smiles.

There was love there, but I kept losing teeth and losing teeth and then my new teeth were worth nothing and my mother wanted to fix them with braces, so we pull out some more teeth and we fix the ones that are still left in my mouth.

My mouth talks funny for the first few weeks. My mother makes me soup and cuts tofu into tiny Lego-sized cubes and asks me questions while I'm trying to chew and I get mad at her but I still love her, and I know this because I write her letters and poems and she writes them back. She goes running with me. She is making me a better person. I clatter after her with my soldered teeth.

Teeth are made for biting, and maybe I forget how to love her when I stop chewing, when I start swallowing, when I start letting men past my gums and down my throat, when I start wrapping my lips around my teeth to obsolete them. But I know that isn't true, because in her presence I pull the fangs out again from where they are stuck inside my veins and we sit together and eat cai png, noisy, I grumble at her for chewing so loud.

My ex thinks I eat weird. We are on Skype and they say I scrape my spoon against the plate too loud, and the way I place food into my mouth is

disgusting! Ew.

Their face is my face when I speak to my mother nowadays, and it hurts because this is the moment I know I have not been loving her. I end the Skype call. I haven't called home in a long time. I've been whitening my teeth.

Who the fuck gets so hung up on teeth?

When I see my mother again, it is for dinner. We swap drinks. She likes the mojito. I don't, but I say I do. She orders another, drinks it with pursed lips. She orders seafood for us to share. I eat the chicken. We are all over the place, eating the wrong things, drinking asymmetrically. She asks the waiter to take a photograph of us. I say I don't really use my phone as much nowadays. She blushes and puts her phone away.

We are caught in a blender, we are a soft food for acid bellies. Love does not taste like porridge, but she asks me to make chog for her. When I am free. When I am not so busy.

I am not that busy. I have time for walking, and roller-skating, and fucking. I have time for cooking, but I don't do it. I don't do it, even though my tongue is still tracing the absence of us, the absence of us, the absence of us. Is this symptomatic of getting older?

She says *I keep forgetting you're an adult now.* I say I'm not. She insists I am. We talk about insurance. Something in her voice breaks and I am aware we are not talking about insurance. We are reaching for the ratty strings of what's left between us. When they say "holding a conversation", they mean it like this, like holding a full bowl of soup with both hands, trying not to spill anything, unsure when you will eat again.

So this is where we are, I muse. Insurance. Our love has been simmering for twenty-two years and the reduction is: insurance. Our love language is her begging me to take care of myself because she's not really sure how to do that anymore. I've bubbled out of her hands, the embryonic sac bursts on impact, I hit the ground running like a manic baby giraffe. She watches with binoculars.

A giraffe's tongue is twenty inches long. I wonder how many times a day it runs across enamel and finds something missing, and then I'm immediately glad I am not a giraffe. My mother is. She is tall and Amazonian and unbreakable and I wonder how I broke out of her in the first place. She should have held on to me, I think. She should never have let me out.

1997. She expelled me from her body and then she tried to keep me. It is confusing to both of us. We sit across the table from each other and I think about how I used to be part of her, how I am a body part she has forgotten. I wonder if she ever runs her hands over the space I used to be. Once upon a time I was the size of a tooth. Now I am big, and I won't fit under her pillow, but here she is, trying to turn me into gold anyway.

There is an ache in the back of my ventricles from thinking about the fact that a baby is a much bigger thing to lose than a tooth. The hole I left behind closes up, shrinks back, but she smiles through the postpartum belly fat and squeezes me into her schedule anyway. When have I ever done the same? I open my mouth a little so I can feel the void that is my entire oral cavity. The mouth is a hole a whole, where you put things when you want to process them. The mouth is where you put things that are too big, and you mash them up until they fit in your body.

A mother is not a tooth. A mother is a soft food to fill the gap she left behind.

My mother asks for the bill and we leave. She asks if I want dessert. I say yes. This time, we sit beside each other. She asks if I want the tiramisu. I say yes.

THE BODY IS A TEMPLE

What? Know ye not that your body is the temple of the Holy Ghost which is in you, which ye have of God, and ye are not your own? (1 Corinthians 6:19)

What? Know ye not that
Mine body is the temple of the Holy Ghost,
That these veins that you drink from course with purified water turned to blood,
The Lord's wine when he eventually kisses me,
Magic on the fingertips of a hypothetical holy man.

What? Know ye not that
Mine body is bedroom unkempt, Queen-sized and full of frogs,
Reptilian prison, all camouflage and toxin,
And the Lord says "let my people go"
But you press poison into my body
So that even I cannot touch it without recoiling.
Know ye not that your body is a sin?

What? Know ye not that
Mine body is untouched, on shelf, stale skin and cavity,
Feel my crevices collect dust on your account
—*let my people go*—Feel my crevices turn to lice,
Crawling sensation of something tickling your head,
You'll roll over in your bedsheets and there I am.

What? Know ye not that
Mine body is the temple of the Holy Ghost,
That the spirit swarms forth when I open my mouth,
Let my people go!
Wild animals become her,
Hot-blooded fury, carnivorous homewrecker.

Stone-cold hearts and a cold stone wall.

Notre-Dame Rebuilding Fund: 850 Million Euros Promised
$1m Grant to Help Restore St Andrew's Cathedral
Singapore's Novena Church Reopens After Multimillion-dollar Renovation

Tell your people that this flesh tomb is risen,
Stone slid away,
Where is the body you tried to bury?
Out defying death and the devil to show Thomas his holes.
Thoughts and prayers raised him once,
The next time he comes it will be for a multimillion cash money donation only.

Know ye not that
Mine body is open for business, that you can watch the
Spirit spill forth if you just tip me enough,
That you can hold out your rod and turn smut into bedbug
If you just subscribe to my OnlyFans,
That you can make my waters flow
If you just get on my premium SnapChat.

The silly Widow gives all she has
Only to watch the temple destroyed in the year 70.
Better to give to a temple that knows its expiry date,
Better to give to a temple that knows it has five years before your tithes slip from between its thighs and into somebody else.

Jesus sits outside my entrance,
Jesus berates me for these transactions,
Jesus flips tables and scatters coins,
Jesus wants to know why I dirtied the house of the Lord.

As if the bodies that enter me are any purer,
As if the bodies that enter me are not dirty from labour,
As if the bodies that enter me are not sluts for the system,
Whores of a class war,
As if the bodies that enter me don't have to suck capitalism's cock if they want to eat dinner,
As if the bodies that enter me asked to be on all fours for Bezos when they went out to be the family's breadwinner,
As if the exploitation is my cross to bear alone,
As if I am the only one selling my body to survive.

Know ye not that
Mine body has been ravaged by a system it didn't ask to be in,

Know ye not that
Jesus dined with the sex workers and called out the priests,
Know ye not that
Sluts go to heaven and capitalists go to hell,
Because Know Ye Not that each body is a temple,
And perhaps my body is made of wood instead of gold,
But if the wood in my eye is paying my taxes,
You best believe the plank in theirs is avoiding paying theirs,
And if the foundations of my temple are sex and lust,
You best believe theirs are built on violence and greed,
And if some of God's seed falls onto barren land,
You best believe they were the ones who made us barren,

Who make us barren,
Perhaps my temple's waters have turned to blood,
But that is only because they have destroyed 75% of the world's water systems,
Perhaps my dust has turned to gnats,
But that is only because they have degraded 75% of the world's soil.
Perhaps my body is only animals and pests,
But that is because they have killed 93% of the earth's plant biodiversity—

You cannot birth new temples when the ground beneath you is dead and infertile,
You cannot lieth carnally with your love when the concept has been copyrighted,
You cannot burn me at the stake for fucking men for money
When the richest men in the world are fucking the whole earth for free.

HE FUCKED ME LIKE THE NORTH-SOUTH LINE

He fucked me like the North-South line.
The air was hot and heavy, the world stood still.
Our bodies collided the way trains do at Joo Koon,
His Marina South Pier against my Redhill,
Marymount me, I am your Chinese Garden.
15 December 2011 had nothing on him,
I was moaning about it for weeks afterwards.

Train is coming, train is coming, train is coming!

But it isn't.
Over the course of 5 years and 11 months,
the MRT has broken down more than 80 times.
We're coming, coming, but never arriving,
He's building new train lines where I never said I wanted them.
He's tearing down my nature reserves,
uprooting my Bukit Brown,
whispering that I'll like it once he's finished.

We apologise for the inconvenience.

But it's okay.
A "bang" is really just us
"coming into contact".
We start to believe it.
Start to believe maybe a
"train fault" will just last seven more minutes,
maybe a "signal fault" just means "miscommunication"
and god, it's that time of the year anyway what with the rain and all so it isn't really
maybe a "track fault" has nothing to do with corporate cultures and bad attitudes and
everything to do with our own time management.
We learn to pencil them into our planners,
add ten minutes on to our journey time in the morning because
who knows what'll happen?
We learn to accept it when our bosses call them "invalid excuses" for latecoming,

learn that it is our responsibility to avoid being affected
by something that was never ours to control.

Love your ride!

But I can't.
Wikipedia calls these breakdowns "ongoing and spasmodic",
and I can't help but think "ongoing and spasmodic"
is how he feels like when he's on top of me and I can't move
and even though I know the train will always grind to a stop at Ang Mo Kio,
it is true that inevitability is no cure for interruption.
He interrupts my day.
We grab onto handrails, let the architecture of the train catch us
as if it isn't the same architecture that won't fucking budge,
we hang on to the cold plastic promise of efficiency.
We normalise the vocabulary of failure

"Even the main media have turned tabloid. Yes, exciting, and so on . . . frightening readers."

This is a PR disaster,
An emergency for men—
all men, not just for the men
who have never caused 28 casualties,
whose body counts are non-existent.
We are taught to be quiet,
listen to them explain away irresponsibility on national TV,
even though it was never their story to tell.
We are taught that a free shuttle service is enough to make up for the fact
that a long history of apathy has led to irreversible system damage.
We are told to forget that
we still can't commute the way we could before.
If we complain,
they can say we're being unreasonable.
"Look what I've given you," he says.
"You should count your blessings."
But I'm too busy counting the number of stops til I'm home,
eyes down, legs together, face red.

He fucked me like the red line.
But I don't know how he managed to,
since he doesn't see lines,
can't see the platform gap between a yes
and my terrified no.
We're getting off at Bartley,
is this something he learned in the army,
this aggression is it something to do with the suspension in the tracks,
there's a lapse in my memory,
will he even remember me,
I barely even know him
but he's now asking me to

He fucked me like the North-South line.
The air was hot and heavy, the world stood still.
Our bodies collided the way trains do at Joo Koon,
His Marina South Pier against my Redhill,
Marymount me, I am your Chinese Garden.
15 December 2011 had nothing on him,
I was moaning about it for weeks afterwards.

When I finally take to the Internet to gripe about my experiences,
I'll be told that other people have it worse.
Singapore is so safe already, what more do you want?
Singaporeans are so 乖[1] already, just bear with it,
Singaporeans are fucking me without my permission,
Making me bare it, you can't tell me what to want.

I am angry, I am the lightning that struck Bedok,
And I will shut down your train lines,
I will be your disruption,
I will make you halt operations for two Sundays because
I am a force to be reckoned with, and
Damn right you should be scared of me,
Damn right you should be apologising,
Damn right your ministers should be terrified.

---

[1] Mandarin for "well-behaved"

I was never a tabloid, I was a diary entry written in untrained cursive,
I was a shaky phone call to a friend, a string of unintelligible text messages,
And when you say I've magnified the problem,
What you really mean is that I've magnified your problem,
That suddenly, the tears on my pillowcase are
Staining your men in green, and their camouflage has stopped
Working.

He fucked me like the North-South line.
The air was hot and heavy, the world stood still.
Our bodies collided the way trains do at Joo Koon,
His Marina South Pier against my Redhill,
Marymount me, I am your Chinese Garden.
15 December 2011 had nothing on him,
I was moaning about it for weeks afterwards.

He fucked me like the North-South line
This is my letter of complaint.

LOCKDOWN FUCKING

In lieu of masturbation,
I will be fucking onions.
Cry fake tears for once.
Fuck something with layers
For once.

In lieu of fingering other people,
I will be sticking my hands in jam.
Tesco will kick me out but
It'll feel good to have sticky fingers again.

I think I'm frozen peas sex,
Essential sex, immortal sex,
Hold me against you when you're hurting sex.
You think I'm produce aisle sex,
Best before sex, easily bruised sex,
Can't eat it by itself sex.

Freezer's broken.
We put 50 variations of potato in the refrigerator,
50 variations of potato going rotten at once
I'll stink up your fresh grapes.

French fry body,
Greasy child of god.
They ate Jesus with wine,
They'll consume me with beer.

Fuck me when you're blackout drunk,
Ask me how many times I've come,
Pull back my hair, whisper your grocery list in my ear
So that I remember what you need in the morning.

ALLY CHUA

PEDIGREE

> "It's wild, when you think about it. These plants love
> to be tortured. The more you manipulate them,
> the more they give."
>
> —Francisca P. Coelho, horticulturist

I'm teaching my child
the art of ozukuri.

How to splice cutting from parent,
tie its stem to splint.

How to throw runt buds away. Shroud plant
in cloth to trick it into sleeping.

This yield and push, this forced
blossoming.

My child is fidgety, biting her nails
to the quick. I pry her fingers from

obstinate lips. I've almost broke her
from this habit, she's growing into her

skin. One day she'll be a
replica of myself.

JUXTAPOSITION OF APRON STRINGS

  to pull on a string &
    feel it resist.

        to unwind a line
        into spun gold.

    to test for
  poisoned apples.

        to eat
        forbidden fruit.

 to unpack a maze,

        to hide within hedges.

   to hold a fist,

       a fistful of sugar.

   to protect
   the princess,

        to bed the minotaur.

   the sum of it,

       in other words,

   to never relinquish control.

MARTIN SCORSESE AND I GET INTO A TAXI

Travis Bickle drives through the streets of New York, set to Bernard Herrmann's jazz soundtrack. The sidewalks are steaming with filth and hellwater. His vision is saturated, burnt reds and neons. He says: *"All the animals come out at night—whores, skunk pussies, buggers, queens, fairies, dopers, junkies, sick, venal. Someday a real rain will come and wash all this scum off the streets."*

#

Tonight I am in Chinatown. The shops are closed, the sidewalks stacked with trash bags. I make my way to Doyers Street. According to *The New York Times*, more people have died at the Bloody Angle, the crook at Doyers Street, than any other intersection in America.[1] Tonight on Doyers Street, it's just me. Tonight is the kind of night that sits quiet, a placeholder time between Monday slog and Friday after hours.

Three nights later, in the same area, a stranger will bludgeon 4 homeless men to death.[2]

#

Couldn't help but imagine—no, not what you think. Not that it could have been *me*. Rather—if I were there, if I had seen it, could I have stopped it? A man bludgeoning sleeping people is not a fair fight. A man who clubs sleeping men is a cowardly man. A man with a hammer is not as dangerous as a man with a gun.

Then the thought: *"Who exactly do you think you are?"*

#

My name is A. I eat healthy, wear sunscreen, and go to the gym regularly. I like cooking, and I know enough about fermenting to recognise what SCOBY is. I can quote *The*

---

[1] Lii, J H (1994, June 12). "NEIGHBORHOOD REPORT: CHINATOWN; on Pell Street, only memories of a violent past." *New York Times*. www.nytimes.com/1994/06/12/nyregion/neighborhood-report-chinatown-on-pell-street-only-memories-of-a-violent-past.html

[2] Sandoval, E., Rashbaum, W. K., Singer, J. E., & Joseph, Y. (2019, October 5). "In Chinatown, rampage against sleeping homeless men leaves 4 dead." *New York Times*. www.nytimes.com/2019/10/05/nyregion/homeless-men-killed-chinatown.html

Godfather, *Goodfellas*, *Taxi Driver*, and other classics. On my days off, I attempt risky things—travel alone, climb mountains, fuck strangers I've just met.

#

"What is your kink? What do you like?"

#

I think about the classic movies I love. The prodigal son and his descent into an empire of ashes. The insomniac and his descent into madness. Robbers holding a bank hostage. Film noir. Mob movies. Here's the common thread—the protagonists are all white males. Another common thread—all women relegated to the background, smoking their cigarettes, swinging their toned calves. The 1970s was a homogenous kind of time for cinema, wasn't it?

#

Or perhaps there is some sort of misogyny innate in me. How I identify more with male characters; how I admire the Shylockian nature of their conflicts. When Michael Corleone said, *"It's not personal, it's just business,"* I felt an admiration that sank deep. When Henry Hill in *Goodfellas* avoided the queue outside a high-end club and navigated through its back-of-house to the lounge, I envied the ease in which he entered that exclusive, selective world.

In those movies they settled disputes over gambling tables and spent the rest of their time smoking long cigars and drinking good whiskey. Their conflicts were deadly but decisive. They didn't mull over, ponder, or second-guess their choices. There was no navel-gazing. Their loneliness was salved by beautiful women. Kay Adams—Michael Corleone's childhood sweetheart. Betsy—Travis Bickle's object of desire.

When I think about these movies, I didn't want to be Kay Adams. I didn't want to be Betsy. I wanted to be Michael Corleone. I wanted to be Travis Bickle.

#

"What is your kink? What do you like?"

#

In the movie *Taxi Driver*, Martin Scorsese makes a cameo as a passenger that Travis Bickle picks up. Martin Scorsese gets into a taxi and says:

> "I have a 44 Magnum pistol. I'm gonna kill her with that gun. Did you ever see what a 44 Magnum pistol can do to a woman's face? I mean, it'll fucking destroy it. Just blow her right apart. That's what it can do to her face.
>
> "Have you ever seen what a 44 Magnum will do to a woman's pussy? Now that you should see."[3]

#

"What is your kink? What do you like?"

#

Well, you want to know.

So let me say this: I want to be helpless. I want to be powerless. I want men to take me by force, wrap their hands around my neck, and choke me until I ride the edge of fear. I want their weight on me.

#

In 2015, I read about Chris Brown's assault on his then-girlfriend, Rihanna. I saw the photo of her battered, bruised face. The police report says:

> ...When he could not force her to exit, he took his right hand and shoved her head against the passenger window of the vehicle causing an approximate one-inch raised circular contusion. Robyn F. turned to face Brown, and he punched her in the left eye with his right hand. He then drove away in the vehicle and continued to punch her in the face with his right hand while steering the vehicle with his left hand. The assault caused Robyn F.'s

---

[3] Movieclips. (2014, January 15). *Taxi Driver (4/8) movie clip - a sick passenger (Martin Scorsese cameo)* YouTube. www.youtube.com/watch?v=X6frLQWOSlQ

```
mouth to fill with blood and blood to splatter all over
her clothing and the interior of the vehicle.

Brown looked at Robyn F. and stated, "I am going to beat
the shit out of you when we get home! You wait and see!"
. . .
After Robyn F. faked the call (for help), Brown looked at
her and stated, "You just did the stupidest thing ever!
Now I am really going to kill you!"
. . .
Brown began applying pressure to Robyn F's. left and
right carotid arteries causing her to be unable to
breathe, and she began to lose consciousness.⁴
```

In 2019, I read about Jennifer Schlecht, senior advisor in the United Nations Foundation, who was decapitated by her husband after she asked for a divorce.

Last evening I read a forum post where a woman shared how her partner started to choke her in the middle of sex until she passed out. He waited until he finished before checking if she was fine.

He had never done that before, she said. They have been together for five years. What should she do?[5]

#

On the other side of the world, I live in an insulated, self-contained world. I run alone, gym alone, eat dinner alone. I shower in a deserted gym, before taking the last train home. I am always safe. Yet I wake up at 2am with nothing and everything on my mind. In New York City, it is 2pm. I can hear the subway trains. I can hear Travis Bickle. *"Twelve hours of work and I still can't sleep. Damn. Days go on and on. They don't end."*

#

---

[4] Los Angeles Police Department. (2009, July). "Search Warrant and Affidavit" (No. 58168). *The Smoking Gun*. http://www.thesmokinggun.com/file/lapd-details-rihanna-beating?page=3
[5] u/throwra_dontbelieve. (2020, May 21). "My boyfriend choked me until I passed out during sex, waited until he "finished" to check on me." [r/relationship_advice post]. Reddit. www.reddit.com/r/relationship_advice/comments/gnq99t/my_26f_boyfriend_35m_choked_me_until_i_passed_out

When I say I travel alone—that I have hiked mountains by myself, slept out of a van alone, trekked solo—I am always asked, first and foremost,

"Is it safe is it safe is it safe?"

\#

I'm not afraid of being by myself, I want to tell them.

\#

Over half of the killings of American women are related to intimate partner violence, with the vast majority of the victims dying at the hands of a current or former romantic partner.[6]
—The Atlantic

Dorothy Stratten, Playboy Playmate, shot by her husband. Nancy Benoit, model, strangled by her husband. Jennifer Schlecht, senior advisor in the United Nations Foundation, decapitated by her husband. April Jace, athlete, shot by her husband. Desirae Parnell, clinic manager, shot by her ex-boyfriend. Dominique Dunne. Ciera Jackson. Sabrina Rosario. Nina Reiser. Janet March. Laci Peterson. Shan'ann Watts. Donnah Winger.

\#

Here's what I know: I am not a victim.

I want to walk down the streets at 3am I want people to move out of my way I want a rise and fall origin story I want to be the tough motherfucker I want to drink hard I want to fuck hard I want to enter the lair of the beast I want to defy the underworld king I want to drive fast I want to be heartless I want to be cruel I want to be a villain I want I want I want.

\#

---

[6] Khazan, O. (2017, July 21). *Nearly half of all murdered women are killed by romantic partners.* *The Atlantic.* www.theatlantic.com/health/archive/2017/07/homicides-women/534306

Some nights I put on Bernard Herrmann's soundtrack. I think about the late nights I wandered the streets of rainy Brooklyn, of snowy Manhattan, inconsequential and invisible in the world. Until I pull off my hat to show I am a woman. Then it becomes:

> "Is it safe is it safe is it safe."

\#

Dear Travis,

I write this to you in the throes of an insomnia I can't shake off. The oblivion I can't walk away from. Nights go on, they don't end. They go on and on and on.

\#

Guilt in the middle of the night. Guilt so much I can't sleep. That everything that makes me feel good—when I am pinned against the door, when the choke lasts a little longer, when the boundaries get blurrier, when I continue loving every misogynistic movie every masculine show I love—when I watch Lars Von Trier—when I read Charles Bukowski—women like me women who like violence women who worship men women who bend to men—are the reasons other women die—I am—guilty guilty guilty.

\#

Some nights I rewatch *Taxi Driver*. I watch this lonely man disintegrate on the streets of New York City. I watch his thoughts go to violence. I watch the women in the background. I rewind to the part in the cab, where the passenger says:

```
"Have you ever seen what a 44 Magnum will do to a
    woman's pussy? Now that you should see."
```

IT HAPPENED AGAIN—

        I woke up to sheep screaming
the apples honeycombed
with worms, each crop as rotten
              as the next.
I tend to the sheep
        until my hands
slip in viscera
        until they stop kicking.

All I want
        is life, ripe
              on the fields
so when I see her
young skin, as smooth as
        malleable clay
I take the reddest apple
I make it toffee sweet
I put out the breadcrumbs
            the gingerbread
labyrinth
the shape of a
trap
        she follows—
        they always follow.
    In the centre, no minotaur,
but spindle and cauldron await.

After that, I took what was
            left of her
I put it under a headstone, like the
other twelve
        before.
Red hood, snow skin,
such horror, you will say

but—

then the trees start budding
& they grow heavy
& the fruits drip
   with sap.
If I should bite down into peach
& find four molars
  or a clump of hair
I'll put them on the mantel
  along with the rest.

LUNAR CYCLE

my body sheds
new life, over &
double.

i was told both
it was sacred,
it was filth—

in other words
godliness i do not
care for.

my folklore says
you could feed a
house spirit with

excised blood
& it shall
bring good luck.

my folklore says
not to enter temples
on the days i bleed.

me, i just wonder
if fresh blood
smells the same

after it's been
hung
for a while.

me, i worry about
life, embedded onto
my unwilling cradle.

let the belly not
give way. let it
stay dead, & dead.

me, i ignore
my body's
grip,

as, fingers bloodied,
i hold up this
cup of viscosity.

like all the gods who
devour their
children

there are worse things
i have killed.

THE BOYS IN THE LINEUP

Suppose one night

when you are ready for bed   your phone rings

                    & it's the

                         police

asking if you could

          identify a boy   from a lineup.

So you head to the station & see them in a row—

your father,   your lover,

     your future son,   &

a ghost you can't quite make out.

Maybe it's in the shape of the boy

     you buried in your yard

                    or the dead weight,

on the other side of the bed.

All of them have seen you nude.

               All of them

     have seen your best side

          & your shadow over them at 4am,

     with a shovel   & a pack of ice.

All of them have flayed you

     from heart to marrow.

                    & you figure out

          who you're supposed to save.

    See,

        all the boys you loved

            have left   so it must mean

        you like broken things.

Like a loose slat of wood

        between your give

                & its yielding

            it's been hollow

                all this time.

Of course it's you to the rescue

                the crime scene clean up.

    & you wonder,

        how long can you

      dust dirt off your hands

          return to

a quiet room,   a cold room,

    without the warmth of bodies or

            their festering stench.

    so.

suppose one night

when you are ready for bed   your phone rings

            & it's the

                police.

They ask, can you—

      identify the body   on the highway

in the hospice,   sign off on the time of death

        collect your heart,   in disembodied

scraps,   returned to sender.

You must swallow

        hard knob in your throat   & touch

mangled mess   you must identify the thing

        it used to be.

You must make the eulogy   & it will go

        all good things must end.   You know this, yet

endings are chapters you refuse to shut.

        Schrodinger's boys

in a box,   in the yard.

    If you try hard enough

maybe they'll come back to life.

                & if they didn't,

      what could be worse,   what could be worse—

suppose one night

when you are ready for bed   your phone rings

            & it's the

                police.

Your daddy   has broke   your mother's jaw

       your son the killer

in the driver's seat   your lover

      a noose   tight around your neck.

     Look at you—
while he dusts the dirt   off his hands
  you worry about the sleep he is not getting.
A monster must know a monster
    so maybe you've hammered him
  into the shape you want.

See, you know this:
  a lineup is not meant to save.
    So, pick him out,
  the boy you could not fix.

  Because this lineup   is you,
cut into parts
   on the other side of the glass.
The only one guilty
  the only one with the shovel
    you are the ghost
    & the last unknown in this lineup.

Suppose one night you just stayed by the phone
  & waited
    & waited
     for the storm to happen.
   For the killing blow.
& the boys in the lineup   they wait.

SHAWN HOO

NATURAL HISTORY OF THE FLORIDS, 19TH CENTURY

TAME

A wilderness into a garden. A word into a gauntlet.
In 1824, the *Fame* flamed off the coast of Sumatra—

    the ship's tail a bright orange
    like the back-wing of a scarlet minivet
    the rest of the deck like the black of a starling
    with each crow member draped and desiccated
    knowing that Noah's ark is sinking and

    —with it: Lady Sophia's harp tuned to E-flat   its throat tightened

        to sing like a celempung   looted palaces in chests   jewels

        jackets   geopolitical correspondences   the map

          of Sumatra like a floating arm   the eye

            of a crested jay shrieking   even other men

              and all his dear drawings   like a boy

                who loses his memory

                of strange animals

                    in strange postures

                all up in flames

              like wild grass

              is where we begin.

CLASSIFY

According to Munshi Abdullah—Raffles employed four men in his vocation:

    one to search for mosses, leaves, and flowers, or nature without locomotion

    another to search for grasshoppers, cicadas, and worms, a micro-world of motion

    a third to look for corals, shells, and molluscs, far more ambiguous in motion

    and finally, wild animals—deer, meaning four-legged—taxied, out of motion.

He classified the men according to such and such a notion.

DESCRIBE

Tapirus Indicus—naming begets a name   for the strange peanut-bodied

creature with a truncated nose   already, this body demands description

Bodies demanding description get described:

> Farquhar spots a Malayan tapir on all fours while he is on the road.
> Farquhar's someone sketches it on all fours, languishing on a road.
> He entraps one (frees one), holds one (folds one), counts every characteristic.
> Farquhar submits the manuscript to the Researches of Asiatick.

Bodies demanding description get intercepted:

> Raffles is looking to acquire this fabled manuscript, he acquires
> the friendship of Pierre-Medard Diard, Alfred Duvaucel, who acquire
> and copy the manuscript by hand, who happen to be French and acquainted
> with Georges Cuvier who publishes what was the first known description.

Bodies demanding description get described:

> Half a century before, the English Orientalist William Marsden lists
> the hippopotamus, or what purportedly in Malay is called kuda ayer;
> Half a millennium before, Ma Huan accompanies Zheng He through mists
> of the South Seas, calls it 神鹿. The divine stag or the water horse?

Bodies demanding description get described by bodies demanding description.

Tapirus Indicus—the name sticks   for the strange peanut-bodied

creature with a surfeit of story   and a truncated trunk

for which we are without indigenous description.

DRAW

Before the camera was a painter.

We do not hear of the Chinese painter

from Macau except that he was an expert in fruits and flowers.

The manggis must have hung so lusciously low, at any moment

it could split from its stem and become real in one's hand.

Before the Chinese painter who painted for the European eye

was the gibbon's vital motion. The pressure of the brush hands

its shadows across skin. The speed of it leaves the wind.

The angle of a brush, a repertoire of bush.

Before Monet perhaps, before Renoir.

NATURAL HISTORY OF THE FLORIDS, 20TH CENTURY

NAME

When Udagawa Yōan uttered *dōbutsu* in 1822
he understood, without knowing, the word *zoo*.

    A word is like a node you place in the field of language   of arable risk
        it lights up near then unnear words then   you lose sight of the node.
    In this case, he placed the word *animal* in the Japanese   and the field echoed

                enclosure.

    Whoever set the Latin aflame with the word *botanica*
    is indirectly accountable for the Japanese *botanika*,

    though not fully. Egbert Buys who wrote his treatise on botany
    in Dutch is responsible for Udagawa's *The Sutra of Botany*,

    if only in part. Equally, the London Zoo,
    in some ungrammared language is an anagram of Ueno Zoo.

    Just yesterday, I heard that weather is akin to river:
    downstream is a drawback, but disaster can swim like salmon

    it's this relationship that we call   *history*, like a node placed
    in the field no river of time   blighting faraway worlds

        repeating the word *enclosure*.

EXHIBIT

As *dōbutsu* births the *dōbutsuen,*
Nanpō births the *Nanpō seitai ten*

    The Southern Ecology Exhibit, Spring 1943
      sought to gather the specimens of the Southern territories
        imagine—   the *Dugong dugon* sleeping under the cherry blossom
                      the bulbous eyes of the tarsier casting aspersions
                      the Asian water monitor made Pan-Asian

      just imagine—   every specimen brought to a microcosm in Ueno

        the little boy whose father is sent to Syōnan points

           at the kancil and sees what his father sees

              not a line of men but a mousedeer

                  a wily mousedeer, he learns,

                      an ungrateful animal

      he holds the map of the zoo and carves
            the territory like a melon with his finger

      circles the animals he wants
            to see, he's heard so much

      and the zookeeper is only happy
            to show him around *Nanpō*

      represented on that ludic map
            he holds—the most natural

      thing in the world—
            a board game

      matching an Asian nationalist
            with an Asian animal.

INVENTORY

IN

three tortoises
three baby crocodiles
a turtle
& a three-month old iguana lizard

> "In **the spacious** gardens surrounding the **Museum**, these reptiles lead a blissful existence, totally unaware **as it were** of the scurry of motor-traffic that passes only **a few feet** from their abode. Two granite basins, originally **hewn for** domestic purposes, provide the tortoises, young crocodiles and the solitary turtle with a place they can call home. **The young** iguana is **housed** in a small wire-enclosed cage **amidst** conditions resembling as closely as possible **his own** native habitat."[1]

OUT

three African zebras
an Australian cassowary
three African cranes
two Australian cranes
& a dove from Nicobar Islands[2]

---

[1] Adapted from "Miniature Zoo Started in Syōnan Museum," *Syōnan Shimbun*, 15 June 1943
[2] Adapted from "Wild Life for Ueno Zoo Given by Johore Sultan," *Syōnan Shimbun*, 1 October 1942

ELIMINATE

>The Abysinnian lions,
>Hakkō the Leopard, led
>by their stomachs, bend—
>>only the elephants kneel
>>at strychnine in sinew.

In the Summer of 1943, Ōdachi Shigeo
    —Mayor of Syōnan, then Governor General of Tokyo—

ordered the massacre of the animals
    —by poison preferably, if not starvation or strangulation—

and by September that year, fourteen species were killed
    —and by 1945, ten million of the species *Homo sapiens*—

and a ceremony for the animal martyrs held
    —the monks intone a sutra *jikyoku sutemi dōbutsu*—

>Did he place the word *massacre* in the field to light the word *defeat*?
>For others, he placed the word *massacre* and lit the word *sacrifice*.

>If order is also about elimination,
>>what did the monks expunge with the word *dōbutsu*?

>And the three baby crocodiles in the Syōnan Museum,
>>who are their descendants?

>And the animals at Punggol Zoo in 1942,
>>the birds shot dead by the British, or released out of fear,

>>>what are their names? Release their names.

NATURAL HISTORY OF THE FLORIDS, 21ST CENTURY

SURVEY

The beach, the rubble, the mangrove,
    the coast, the seagrass, the shore

        —their activism rose

            like a cape on the south-eastern tip of an island

              at the eleventh-hour, rose

                  at the close of a strenuous century

                      rose like cliffs I've seen in Galway

                          rose against the main
                              landlocked scape.

Those who were close say Chek Jawa crept up unannounced,
when plans to reclaim land for military uses were announced.

Already the bulldozers were dozing like bulls in the barnacles.
Already the cranes glistening beside the crustaceans were eager.

Chek Jawa once sat like an ascetic who'd renounced his throat.
Chek Jawa saw a pair of Krauncha birds shot through their throats
                                      —and sang

                for the carpet anemones rhyming
                with the sponges; for the spider crab
                believing it is both; for the lunges
                of the mud crab and the sea stars,
                for their dreaming in loaves; for the octopus;
                the flatworm; the tunicate; for the nud-
                ibranches ironing their polka dot
                bottoms; for the seaweed strangled
                and fans itself loose; for the mudskipper
                and the little dipper; for the chorus
                that even the dugongs have joined; for

Here is a world in commotion.
Here, any parliament moves its own motion.
Here, we might be moved to our own motion,
      to retain what is
Here: what is manatee, what is matinee,
      what is matter.
Here, no elsewhere.
Here, an island incites us to our song
            —and we sing

      We, the surveyors.
      We, the petitioners.

RECORD

After Eric Lin's Remember Chek Jawa *(2007)*

An island needs its own mythologies.
Hand-held camcorders write our histories.

      Hand-held, we couldn't right our history:
      our disenchantment turned to apathy.

Our re-enchantment began with anemones
closing up their mouths like the Astomi.

      Close-up: and the mouthless Astomi
      turn to Xingtian's defiant mouth-belly.

To turn the city's defiant mouth and belly
towards Chek Jawa—our cameras have no relief.

      To our Chek Jawas, then, our cameras. No relief
      for an island finding its own mythology.

RALLY

Democracy teaches us nothing
but the choreography of bodies.

On a field, each one of us stands
like the dry roots of a mangrove

      at low-tide.   Every body occupies space.   Every body faces an other body.

      Ergo, every body faces away from some body.   A body bodes us to other bodies.

      A body an abode for that other body.   A body aborted a body remains a body.

      And a bold body bodies other bodies to one body.   A body that bodies.

      Bodies bother other bodies.   Body boding bodies.   Bodybuilding bodies.

Heading home from the rally,
staring at that photograph, I know this:

It's the bus we choose to board every morning.
That a bus is one way of reordering bodies.

DEFERRED SAYINGS FOR THE NEXT CENTURY

擔沙填海—了戇工
Carrying the sand to fill the sea—a fool's work
   —a Hokkien saying

Caddying the Sandman to filter the shit—a follower's wern.
Chin-chai the syntax to fulsomate the sayang—aphasia wanze!
Commie the salariat to festoon the scaramouch—a Figaro witling!
Commodus the Sacerdotalist to filibuster!—the sauf a familial wee.
Cambodia the Singapore to fax the simulacra—a phallic wisteria!
Committing the sin to—fuck the sin! A fag's wanion.
Cunard the Succedanea to Fulham the Steinweg!—a factious waiting.
Cantillate, "The Schistous!" to fabiform the sedition—a facial walkie-talkie.
Caliban: "The syncrete to fumigate the speech!"—a fertility's wrackful.
Conditioner the sebum to follicate the scalp—a faux wig-wearer.
Come the shop to find the self—a fervent whichsoever.
Colonialist, the Stamford to forcipate the Success—a fair word!
Contain the scaturient to foreclose the sensifacient!—a foeticide writing.
Coddling the students to free the secession—a forfex wending!
Chemise, the sartorial to follow the straitjacketing—a fashionable wariness.
Combinant the sayings to frictive the slang—affective witticisms.
Cack the cyberspace to frack the solution—a facia Wikipedia.

THERE

There is a land you have learned all your life to desire to go to. No one you know has been there. Not your brother who is still too young to. Not your parents who from their own not having been there built a path on their backs that lead there. No one but a cousin you've heard who went there but came back having not liked where they have been to. Let alone live there. You go there. You were told by the people who have been there that you have what it takes to not just go there but to live there. They spoke of this place highly unlike your cousin whom you've heard hardly spoke since she came back of when she's been there. You believe of course the people who spoke highly of this place because other people spoke highly of the people who hadn't just gone but lived there. That's right, you were told by the people who had lived there that you could live in a place like nowhere. And so you live there. First the people welcomed you who had what it took to not just go but live there. First you learn the people who had lived there believed you lived there. First you learn there are those like you who have learned to want to live there and are there. First you learn of others who always lived there without going anywhere. First you learn the language of there and love the language of there. First the language loved you back and you learn why people loved to say that you could always live there. First you call it there. First you call home and spoke so highly of how you really now live there. First you tell your parents who wanted you to live there how lovely everything was how they should come there. First they say they will of course they will but later you learn that what they meant was not what you meant when we said come there. First they came to go there not to live there. First you resented that they could not live there. All your life they had wanted from their own not having been there to go there for you to go there and now that you are there won't live there. All your life you have learned to desire to go there and now you in your own words want to live there. First the language loved you back you hold the language so tight the other one breaks. Always you call it there although you live there. Like you always lived there you'll always live there. The people who have learned to love there start to tell you that proverbially *first the language loved you back you hold the language so tight the other one breaks*. A proverb is what people who have lived there agree to love there. All your life you call home to find what's holding you back. All your life you call to say how much you love it there. All your life yes they love me too yes even that even the language loves me yes. All your life you call home saying less and less. Soon you'll be living inside a dictionary.

YOU WANT TO WRITE A SENTENCE AS CLEAN AS A BONE

—James Baldwin

Fat congeals
to the bone. I have
written an overgrown
melon and the wheelbarrow
will not budge. Rotund
with redundancy, it
isn't much. Footnotes
gather at its tendrils
like a sink of black hair.
There are ways to sell
oblique and oblong fruit.
If only this wheelbarrow
will move, I might get it
over. Ripe something new.
Tomorrow, no one might
watch over my shoulder,
watch my poem
fatten like a prized goose.
There is not a kernel
of truth in this.

PLACARD

To know this country
is to not know placard

from public assembly.
Not know smiley

from sully. Not know
the difference between

the mirror and myself
and Marxist.

In this museum
without her critics,

politicians fill object
labels, frame the everyday

in its wary diction:
Duchamp's urinal

a mouth to entrap
men soliciting

sperm. A gold staircase
dreams of climbing itself

out of its lease. Reading
on trains translate

to proselytising. So many
misgivings, I want to

assure them: there is more
in my world than me

and my rejoinder to you.
Let down your guard,

paranoid boxer. This poem
is and isn't about you.

ODE TO THE PUBLIC TOILET

Blessed be the stained urinals passing for high windows. Blessed be

the saints you make out by staring at these panes. Blessed be the view

of priests' hats and bald queens. Blessed be the conscientious men

who shake them dry. Bless he who practices personal hygiene in public.

Bless the lewd looks. Bless the tight jeans. Bless the other bodies

swimming in and out of view. Bless darkness. Bless the ungoverned

park which holds this toilet like a cup holds water. Bless the water

fixture for its background pleasure. Pleasure—bless her. For a man

walks in like a stray tune into an empty hall, searching for another

voice, and is blessed with noise. Bless the man that comes

to each cubicle and knows which confessional sputters

forth which sin. Blessed be the boy who puts his ears on the panel

hoping to receive something. Blessed is the man with age whose value

climbs with the night. Blessed is he who comes once, and leaves

three others pining. Bless the mouth. The toe. The lobe. The foot.

The fetish. The fold. The jaw of the man—the man whose knuckles

bled you for daring to want him? Bless him for teaching rejection

with a human punch. Bless the sight of him kissing his knuckles, and count yourself blessed he was no undercover. Bless those who taught

you how to spot an undercover. Bless the men who finally acquired

names—one night, this gift, like a proposal. Bless him for acquainting

you with other blessed men. Bless the less lonely, bless the blanket

of a cheap hotel. Bless cheap hotels built beside parks. And bless the man who opts

for sex in public. Who knows a tap is not a tap

without a shoulder. Who finds friction arousing. Who strolls

all night for nothing

but to leave the scent of his publicity—not scroll

all scentless night into nothing. Bless he

who knows a grid is not a public square

—it is nowhere. We have no one.

IZYANTI ASA'ARI

RUBIK'S MESS

This body is a Rubik's cube, and I have never liked puzzles, the smugness of making things whole when what I want is to hold her, no hurl her against the closest plaster wall, anything that will give more satisfaction than the endless reconfigurations of four-digit numbers on receipt chits to enter rooms to receive answers that are nothing more than educated guesses from persons far more educated than I and that is the truth is it not, none of you thought I would be sitting here, the degrees of unlikelihood multiplied and expressed by testimonials five, and yet I am defiance of demographic, of age race tropicality tumour cell-type, each time this body caught you wrapped you tripped you in a corner unexpected

>   and what corner has not been mangled,
>   each tile plucked and given a file labelled with string,
>   the letters and numbers that dangle to draw lines,
>   to quarter, to suspend hope.

Four cores of tissue sank in formalin
Gross description, core biopsy, 6:00
Specimen NB21-28220, processed in one block
Invasive nests found, tissues snatched

>   You will hear a bang
>   A what?
>   A bang, like a staple gun

It will hurt
Like falling down, he says,

>   (Wrong.)

They have found me,
carcinoma
in-situ

>   now multiple planes
>   unfold.

PARTING WORDS

I.
Be careful where you go,
What your hands reach for

And what they do.
Don't clutch in your hands

What may be carried into the wind,
Lest it is flung back upon your nose.

When you are old,
You will understand.

My grand-daughter, my anak-cucu.
You are perfect. Sempurna.

It is the world that is cruel,
The currents that take no heed.

Listen, listen.
Dengar sini.

Jangan memberontak.
Yang jahanam kita.

Do not fight takdir. Quell your protest.
It is you that will be destroyed.

II.
Grandmother, nyai,
Let me be the destroyer.

They will not believe my words,
And the snakes that lick my ear,

They come without invitation.
It does me no pleasure to see what I see,

How the cards will fall, a few hands down,
In the days, weeks, and months.

I only want to help.
I only want to warn.

I only want to say, stop.
Nyai let me unfurl my tongue,

With my blackened skin,
In the shadow of your silenced voice.

I will swallow the blood-seed.
Bring death to the gates.

It was always there.
I will clear the field for you, as you walk.

AFTER THE MOUNTAIN

Hold this fragile wrist
over bone and moving skin,
as I brush my lashes against a pillow.
It is the same sound as a hand against a clock.

Sleepless, my skin warms the bed.
The wings of a moth waiting
for inertia to crest.

Then I remember how once
you said to someone I was the sun
your world revolves around,
and I nodded and accepted it as fact.

I slouch now feeling the weight of
the Grand Canyon in my hands,
my feet swollen with lead.

When the distance stretches and aches,
cellophane pulling tight across
these tensing shoulder blades—
I am looking for light to bring within.

What is the shape of yearning
when articulated in a face?
In mine, the calm of a placid lake,
to echo the sky overhead.

IN THE DESERT, A WOLF

Temperatures run too hot, too cold.
Salt flats go past cheekbones,
the air is arid, and the sand in my eyes
grate against everything.

Come pull your wool over me, you wolf-crying boy;
visit me, dressed in the skins of nylon-sheathed lambs.
Spin the fleece from which you wear,
make me a scarf, a blindfold, and now, run.

Slide the fuzz over these eyes;
I see you slip into the dunes,
hunting.

CREASE

On some days I leave for work
with creases still pressed to my skin,
marks of the unarticulated clinging in
      to this crease that adorns
my brow, in permanence from bedsheets
sullied with too much sleep
—tonight, tonight, I feel the need
to press my face against another,
      if only to stop myself from gritting
my teeth so hard.

THE BOULDER THAT SWALLOWS YOU

Batu belah, batu bertangkup, [1]
the boulder will swallow you whole.

Throw the crown! Soothe the seas.
Pick up the mantle and feel its heft
rust-sharp, its mineral teeth grazing skin.

Batu belah, batu bertangkup,
the boulder will embrace you.

Roots will grow, slow and deep.
The banyan tree hanging overhead
will hold its peace, as marks cut into air.

Batu belah, batu bertangkup,
the boulder engulfs you.

Upon the river, an embankment of steps,
a pleasant tessellation that calls for ease,
cunning and calm.

Batu belah, batu bertangkup,
the boulder splits.

Your thighs tense as you make your way down,
each step ungainly, a breath too-short.
A hierarchy of meters now unsteady.

---

[1] *Batu Belah Batu Bertangkup* is a Malay folktale made into a film in 1959. A mother is betrayed by her greedy son and her daughter's failure to stop him. Running into the forest, the mother cries to be swallowed whole by a boulder and disappears. The phrase has since become the rallying call of aggrieved Malay mothers when slighted by their own brood.

The body absorbs then what it needs to know:
be cautious here, be mindful here,
be still, do not run.

See how each square spans exactly two
and a half strides. Be careful, my son.
There have always been tricks embedded in stone.

THE CITY HAS A REQUEST

City of subsumed desires telling me,
"Let's iron out our differences."
In good faith, I listen,
though I have nothing to say
to smooth words hiding steel intent.

The city does not have guns here,
not in common hold.
Some bullets you swallow
with the warm glass of water
placed in your hand.

Let me take a walk through
the squared parks instead,
place my ear to the trees,
the ones quickly grown,
with shallow roots.

They are the ones listening
to the white noise of trains
tunnelling through soil and rock.
Let them tell me instead
what is being carved here.

DOORWAY

The person has left,
just the house remains.
The person has left,
but the house remains.

When we first move, difficult.
The kampong last time,
the room all so lapang.
He very picky, 3-room, 4-room, all don't want.
Everything too small, sempit, cannot breathe!
Then suddenly, this one,
kat Jurong. Cun-cun. Dapat.
When we move in that time,
so empty, nothing around.
Ni, the floor, batu, marble,
sejuk, sedap. Kalau hari panas,
tak rase, boleh tido. Tak pakai air con.
But my tulang now dah tua. Old.
Sejuk, sakit. Dah lama rumah ni kosong.
Ya la, your father duduk here on his own.
You also kan, dulu?
Window all never open.
Chair tilam table all cover white kain,
all got dust. Sapu lidi in the cupboard
like never use before.
Just now your cousin play,
macam Halloween gitu.

Orangnye dah pegi.
Tinggal rumah je.
The old man has left.
But the house remains.

THE HORIZON BENDS

You tickle the water with your toes,
urging the tide in with
a lightness

that thins the breeze. It whispers through
fingers, both yours and mine,
gentle and faint,

so when the horizon squints, I laugh lightly,
lightly, I borrow your laughter,
to say nothing.

These are the soft tidal waves, grass growing overlong.
Forgive me, I slide past your words at times,
you tell me too much.

I caress your hair in the day, and in the evening,
where my hand hovers to catch the damp.
Between the winds,

You are quiet.
Nyai penat?[1] I ask.
Yes, you say, *yes.*
Nyai nak minum air?[2]
Nyai nak tengok TV?[3]
Nyai dah cukup makan?[4]

Over and over, I hover,
the waves drawing in,
back and forth.

---

[1] Grandmother, are you tired?
[2] Grandmother, are you thirsty?
[3] How about TV?
[4] Will you eat a bit more?

Mapping for more detail, I cast the line,
though not much holds. I am trying
to catch the moon.

Tell me, when does the tide come in?

Let it be sea breeze that catches your hair,
to graze the quiet pearls that
droop from your ears.

LUNE LOH

I WAS BLUR AND FORGOT WHEN MY ASSIGNMENT WENT

The Kraken, in a fog / stories/history/myth/legends set in sea-mist / lens wipe / lens tide / photographic-lack / lack as a / teary-eyed / diffraction of diffraction as distortion / Icelandic Hero imparts sea-knowledge to archivist (Anonymous author, 12??) / sea as a steamed mirror / steamed shoals of merchant ships / of gone civilizations (Verne, 1870) / of Tennyson (1830) / greater than their thirteen-meter squid spawns (ibid.) / only a sonnet that engulfs shipcrew is real / only a horror in undersea mirages / fear limping in confusion / sailors in confusion about measurement / of a sea-mountain / of a dark continent / their dark descendants off Temasek (Wong, 2043, p. 152) / Orang Sotong split from Orang Laut (p. 154) / fish-eyed academia / historical astigmatism / oil-refinery sabotage / Jurong Island arsons / in a fog / container ships / new merchant ships / arm-tentacles still lie in wait / in shadows / in manuscripts lost at sea

LEFT BREAST (TAKE 1 – TAKE 5)

I.

Take your left breast,
fold it into the pocket
of your missing chest.

II.

Take what's left of the
silicone left in breast:
the acquaintance a
star-stain; tumor-scar.

III.

Turn left onto main body
<- Take a right turn at
excavated ribsection ->
no destination abreast

IV.

So, I've taken that I've counted to four:
counted breasts on I & III, how they drooped;
counted breasts on II & IV, how they sounded
better, on the back-bone, on the missing-beat.
I learned them, left behind: direction; notation.

V.

◁-breast as ▲-ing:
▽-pocket, ◸-sound.
Tuned to take empty.

X1 RIGHT-BREAST-PAD (PINKISH, SILICONE, ATTACHED)

I-form (in) plastic / extension-corpus (outside) mould / asked-worship, carved Goddesses distilled (via) syringes / plastic-transition / search-parameter: "beauty" (via) / hyperlink.witchcraft (via) / markup (against) flatchest / burned breast-spine-stake / am mixedmedia / am canvas-sacrifice / Taobao (via) body-temple / body-rash ritual / van-der-waals-skin phenotype / I-construct (against) organic crepe-cream layer / pour-me (inside) / flesh-enabled embed (onto) curse / embed (into) hyperreal-hex / I-transact (out) love

BREATH AS CINEMA

| | |
| , |
.	.
, ,	, ,
; ...	... ; , , -
...	... -
" " .	: , , –
.	(: , ,
–	' ', .
" " " ... ; ; ".	; ; ;) , ; ;
(,), , .	. ( ).
–	.

FEMME DIALECTICS: A PROCESS

/ -as it was imperative / as it was indecisive / as if a decision by a scion / as if a scorpion extension: the regard of a double-claw / double-bind: the finding of the divine / on a clear night, it was allowed for the vines to drip wine / yet a wine of the ocean, dissolving strata / into data / the fermata of the anti-border that burns bolder / either the Queen of the Night or the Queen of the Day turns over / into ordination / into sublimation / the double-she's an indignation / of which variable deltas flow / of which there exists possibilities / of which are snow / of which are now- /

SLEEP PARALYSIS AS LUCID DREAMING

#1

The night river reflected you instead of the gibbous.

#2

In the first dream, I didn't understand anything about you.

#3

In the second dream, I didn't understand me.

#4

and during Autumn it was hot and sunny and we wore red lipstick at the same time without each other knowing and i wanted to kiss you but there were many thoughts that didn't happen at the same time there were many scenes that were staged and it was just me sweating and smudging lipstick with tears at my own cue in the event you died and wanted it and

#5

In the first dream I powdered moonsoil on my face and sent you letters that arrived too late. Everything in retrospect is a dream forgotten five minutes after waking. The sheets hugged your body in rigor mortis instead. I woke up every morning dying, thinking of your corpse preserved in makeup.

#6

Your cocktail layers / how I can't drink / liquids immiscible / into each other / our legs failing to melt / spaces that miss / spaces to miss / you straining my second dream / you pouring ice / me on the rocks thinking of sunrise / you rimming salt on my torn lip / how I reserved a second barstool / but you over the counter / I can't drink my second dream / I can't sleep on this river / drowning in your shaker / so cold / so layered / in your evening hours / I drink and miss / and missed

#7

Three times that week,
we ate our bland voices
and I couldn't apologize;
and we never dreamed.

MALL WORLD

I'll die I'll die I'll die I'll die I'll drink I'll drink I'll drink I'll drink I'll drink I'll die I'll drink I'll drink I'll drink I'll drink I'll drink I'll eat I'll eat I'll drink I'll eat I'll eat I'll eat I'll eat I'll eat I'll die I'll drink I'll eat I'll drink I'll eat I'll drink I'll eat I'll drink I'll eat I'll drink I'll shop I'll drink I'll shop I'll cry I'll shop I'll shop I'll shop I'll shop I'll shop I'll shop I'll shop I'll cry I'll shop I'll shop I'll shop I'll shop I'll shop I'll shop I'll shop I'll shop I'll shop I'll drink I'll shop I'll drink I'll shop I'll drink I'll shop I'll drink I'll shop I'll drink I'll shop I'll drink I'll shop I'll drink I'll shop I'll drink I'll shop I'll cry I'll cry I'll eat I'll eat I'll eat I'll eat I'll eat I'll eat I'll eat I'll eat I'll eat I'll eat I'll eat I'll eat I'll eat I'll eat I'll eat I'll eat I'll shop I'll eat I'll shop I'll eat I'll shop I'll drink I'll eat I'll shop I'll drink I'll eat I'll shop I'll drink I'll eat I'll shop I'll drink I'll eat I'll shop I'll drink I'll eat I'll shop I'll drink I'll eat I'll shop I'll drink I'll eat I'll shop I'll drink I'll shop I'll drink I'll shop I'll shop I'll shop I'll shop I'll shop I'll shop I'll shop I'll shop I'll shop I'll cry I'll shop I'll shop I'll shop I'll shop I'll shop I'll shop I'll shop I'll shop I'll shop I'll shop I'll shop I'll shop I'll shop I'll shop I'll shop I'll shop I'll shop I'll shop I'll eat I'll shop I'll eat I'll shop I'll shop I'll eat I'll die I'll eat I'll eat I'll eat I'll eat I'll eat I'll eat I'll eat I'll eat I'll eat I'll eat I'll eat I'll eat I'll eat I'll eat I'll drink I'll drink I'll drink I'll drink I'll eat I'll drink I'll drink I'll drink I'll eat I'll drink I'll drink I'll drink I'll eat I'll drink I'll eat I'll drink I'll eat I'll drink I'll drink I'll cry I'll eat I'll cry I'll eat I'll cry I'll eat I'll eat I'll eat I'll eat I'll cry I'll eat I'll cry I'll eat I'll drink I'll cry I'll eat I'll eat I'll cry I'll drink I'll eat I'll cry I'll eat I'll cry I'll drink I'll eat I'll cry I'll drink I'll eat I'll drink I'll eat I'll drink I'll eat I'll drink I'll eat I'll drink I'll eat I'll drink I'll eat I'll drink I'll eat I'll drink I'll eat I'll shop I'll shop I'll shop I'll shop I'll shop I'll shop I'll shop I'll shop I'll shop I'll shop I'll shop I'll die I'll die I'll die I'll die I'll die I'll die I'll die I'll die I'll die I'll die I'll die I'll die I'll die I'll die I'll die I'll shop I'll die I'll shop I'll die I'll eat I'll die I'll eat I'll die I'll eat I'll die I'll die I'll shop I'll die I'll drink I'll die I'll die I'll die I'll die I'll die I'll shop I'll shop I'll shop I'll shop I'll shop I'll shop I'll shop I'll shop I'll shop I'll shop I'll eat I'll eat I'll shop I'll eat I'll drink I'll cry I'll shop I'll eat I'll drink I'll cry I'll shop I'll eat I'll drink I'll cry I'll drink I'll eat I'll shop I'll shop I'll live I'll die I'll die I'll die I'll die I'll die I'll die

MOOD AS SPACETIME ERRATA PT. 2

I fall through 4 dimensions:

    (flesh,,, dialectic, pain. and

).

Even,,,,, that society counts my days,: each layer a thin/film. I lie exposed: $_0 0^0{}_0$.
The State performs a twirl on my body^{staged} – it glimmers$^{\text{eyes, eyes, eyes}}$ in the sun$^{\text{eyes, eyes, eyes}}$.

while
    I go to theatre to debug my body$^{\text{stage, set, flesh-prop}}$
    I go to theatre to debug pathos in loops
    I go to theatre to debug my face the $_{\text{eyes}}$state the State^{eyes} recognizes the $_{\text{eyes}}$state recognizes the State
    I am debug-theatre,,, of spacetime-putty
    def the compiled reeling into spatial-error(eyes):
        while
            if $_{\text{eyes}}$eyes^{eyes}
                return body$^{\text{stage, set, flesh-prop, eyes, 0, angle, shot, expression, bug, static,}}$).

SHOU JIE ENG

EIGHT DIVERS

I. Whalemen's Shipping List. New Bedford, Vol. I. No. 4.

Fourth of the month, TUESDAY MORNING, 1843. Vessels out of New Bedford—74. Sailed one to four years since, the earliest having departed in the May of '39. Bound for— the PACIFIC, the N.W. COAST, NEW ZEALAND, NEW HOLLAND (someone has marked *Obsolete—today Australia*). Last report—hailed, gammed, sighted, spoken to, all well, no date, lat. 55 S., long. 72 E., no place, no place—

                                    bound home—
And the oil (*the oil!*)—sixteen,
twenty-six, twelve,
and fifteen hundred bbls. sp.
                                    (*sperm whale—head case oil*)
and at least triple that in wh.
                                    (*whale—non-specific; ordinary blubber*)
At thirty-three bbls. per fish
this paper makes
                                countless
bodies. Chain them by their tails,
that they might fill the casks. See
the way the barrels line
up on Merrill's Wharf, humped
and beached, barks
stirring at the moorings,
merchants circling like crozes.
Gauger, pray you unstop the bung,
dip your rod into the cavity and judge
its contents unflaggingly
sweet and handsome.

II. Whalemen's Shipping List. New Bedford, Vol. XVIII. No. 18.

Rows of type ring out reports of brooding voyages:
        the bark *Lafayette*, spoken to at sea last November with twelve hundred bbls. of
        sperm oil—the *Abigail*, seen four months ago at Oahu, bound home with sixteen—
        a Lady and her son, Wishing to obtain passage to join her husband at Honolulu—
Walter Westervell of Poughkeepsie, aged about twenty-three, killed by whale during hunt.

                In New Bedford the price of oil continues to rise
                (*One hundred and forty-one cents per Gal., 1860*)
                as light-houses and street lamps burn their valuable welcome
                interminably into the fog,
                the Howlands and the Rodmans press their luxuriant candles, soaps, &c.,
                and somewhere in the Pacific
                a whale is unrolled, feeding its flesh to the fire.

III. Attachment

Chains for tillers, stud-link Chains for flukes and fins—
        should any Chain be wanted of given
weight or size, it will be furnished at short notice by
        J. & T. DURFEE, Manufacturers of wrought iron and
certain steel: fences, vaults, edge tools, and whale craft—
        meaning implements for catching fish.
Catching, as in harpooning, lancing, scarfing, cutting-in,
        driving iron into foaming body;
body, as in case oil, ambergris, and blubber, cut into
        blanket and horse, minced into book or bible;
as in raw material, slippery with blood and fat, as in
        product, as in
sold on reasonable terms, of superior quality, and with
        punctuality of dispatch.

IV. Dyer & Co., Coopers.

Dear old beast, dear shaving horse: smell of
stave blanks roughed and stacked on racks,
mist on dust-laden breath. Your back rounded
by the insides of working thighs. Lower your head,
riderless, as if to drink from the cold cresset
in your pen. A fire used to burn all day
in the corner, drawn by wooden air and driven
by a cooper's hope. Grandfather's. His tools still
on the wall, traces of labouring in the handles
of so many backing knives, their edges sharp as
his. You can see it in the way he shed workers
after fights. His children. You can see it in the way
the adzes, chivs, and planes lined up all around
the shop, and the way the roof beam sagged
after he put down his hands.

V. Hands

To reduce the threat of collisions with endangered whale species, vessels sixty-five feet or greater in length shall be slowed to speeds ten knots or less in management areas.

Local reports lament each ship strike. Compliance papers, their bold faces tacked to boards, flutter keenly in the wind. Only yesterday, hands stood, calling out sightings from nests, thrusting lance after lance into ribboned flanks from the bows of thirty-foot boats. Hands making fast the small of the whale, narrowing between fluke and fin. Able hands flensing the fish, the tips of their craft sharpened to eloquent points. Green hands severing and bailing the head case. Sun-dark hands, singed from trying out of oil.

Today, when the whale dives, my friend, a biologist, tracks its depth and marvels at its length. Two hundred metres and twelve minutes, reported in jerks and snatches, charting ragged points on screen. I visit with the friend. She keeps a skeleton model on her shelf, and I notice its carpals, metacarpals, and phalanges—hands, too, five digits within the blade of its fin.

VI. Fishing

I knew a girl from the Cape once, her skin sleek with neoprene, dive flag red and white over the Jonah crabs in her catch bag. When we ducked under it was equilibria. Eelgrass tips pointing up to meet our breaths, gas-pocket haze of unknowing. Further out and fin black, she speared tautogs in two-minute breaths. She asked me to go out whale watching with her. She pulled on the cord, and I followed.

VII. Boatyard, Before the Whales

Planking is in the body as your skin
        is in the sail, latitudes
in the waterlines of your ribs, and longitudes
        the stations of your spine.
Deep draughtly: we explored buoyant
        submergency one summer,
splining fairs across lead ducks and keeling
        over sheer stems. Loft your hull
on the floor, batten to batten: we found
        and marked points a', b', c',
d', e', and so on, intersecting corrections,
        flexing for adjustability.
Slight inaccuracies may have crept in
        during the section, we remembered,
before remembering again:
                jigged cuts, tooth
                gullet, thick
                for planking subtractions.

VIII. How to Say Attachment

Say make fast, or darting. Plant iron, drag
        to impede free motion, pay out
lines, prevent fouling. The rope flies
        after its leader into salt air and
Arctic water. A whale's body knows
        from forward motion where the line
goes, even as it vanishes from sight. Laid hemp,
        held taut by pain and the sear
of the barb. The whaleman casts his drug
        into a child, not to kill it
but to secure the mother. Fastens the calf
        until they have secured the cow.
At home, her belly changes beyond
        seeing, swells against the covers,
child behind her bilge. Find a way
        of saying *attachment*.

MIRABILIS

Piscina: reservoir, miracle unseen,
holding spring flows in aisles of
five by thirteen, walls retaining, columns
proofed in clay and tempered with lime,
waiting—waiting, damp-dark
with time; feet on old stairs, new steps,
descending voices on ancient brick,
young eyes adjust to lamp-lit ears
that trick of water remaining on stone,
net-like steel members standing
not alone but in tandem, instead,
grasping like the roots of trees
an underworld: a Roman fleet no longer
in port, the knees of aqueducts left over;
a vaulted roof the ground for voices
of a different sort.

HOW WE BUILD
(WHEN WE KNOW HOW)

I've been eyeing a carriage house, she tells me, late one night. I see a house in the dark, full of carts without horses or humans. There is a painter on the second floor who is moving out. He is not there when we visit, but the space still has his scent. Whites and blues on the plywood floors, paced into uncertain greys. Tape marks on the walls. Racks, nearly empty, out of two-by-fours with their lumber stamps left on.

*

She wants me to draw up the apartment for her. It will be on the second floor of the carriage house. She wants a large kitchen to cook in and friends to be with her as she cooks for them. She wants a six-foot tub with a good back so that she can soak fully and sit up. She wants to replace the hanging work lights. She wants to keep the timber frame. She wants the light from the three p.m. sun to fall on the curve of her back, where her spine dips between her shoulders at her desk.

*

The second floor is not large, which is why it has not sold. I show her two options for a bedroom given the limited space. She surprises me by asking about flexible living environments. She brings up *critical Italian architecture from the 1960s*. I remember when she hated talking about architecture and architects. *You're all so full of shit*, she retorted once. *You're so full of shit*, she meant. We talk, now, of soft surfaces and bedrooms. The give that a mattress has when you sit down heavily and let yourself fall backwards in frustration.

*

Every client is not a lover. Not every client is a lover. But in some way, all clients are lovers.

*

In a flexible living space, millwork becomes key. Cabinets become closets, become tables, become shelves, become screens. You walk through a door. You walk into a wall. We talk about folding, turning, hiding, reciprocity. The language of everyday things loaded with meanings. Find yourself face to face with your *selves* when you close a door-wall, unable to look away. You pause, remembering, in the pantry-hall.

*

She tells me she will build out the interior herself. Lays out and frames the stud walls, toenailing each vertical member to the bottom plate, heading out the doors, and tying the assembly together. The pencil in her hand marks a piece of spruce-pine-fir. A circular saw pauses, its foot resting on top of the lumber as she sights her mark. Her finger closes on the trigger; the blade comes to life.

*

She starts on the millwork. I help to receive a plywood delivery at the shop, loading the sheets onto the table saw. She sets each sheet on the cross-cut sled, halving an eight-foot panel into two four-by-fours. Her hand grips the crank that raises the blade and turns. Teeth emerge from the throat of the saw. The language of the saw is an uncomfortable thing: the throat is a hole that does not truly exist. Look in any manual. You will find the throat plate covering up the gap. You will find every set screw described with a name and number. But you will not find the void itself.

*

Do you think the throat has a voice? she asks. A quiet voice, like the sigh that the saw makes when you push the piece against the blade, taking it momentarily out of plane. A difficult voice that you feel when the work kicks against you. An expansive voice, like a singer's, at ease through the larynx. The shop floor hums as she feeds the plywood over the plate.

*

Superstudio and Archizoom are the collectives most people think of when they think of *critical Italian architecture from the 1960s*. The work of Superstudio is a work of figures and grids. Bodies—naked and clothed, cities, dogs and cows, friends, families with a child, or many, parties, protests—are enmeshed in hashes of lines. The unit of the grid is scaleless, and the grid runs on to infinity. In a proposal, Superstudio dreamed of damming the flow on the American side of the Niagara Falls, temporarily, as the Army Corps of Engineers did in the summer of 1969, to build a rectangular basin with a mirrored, stainless steel finish. The flow would then be restored, and water would thunder back into the basin, filling it up in *33 minutes, no seconds, and 94 hundredths*. During that time, water and reflected sky would touch, throatless.

CHRISTIAN YEO

REFUGE

Say we met at the border,
where the man hides behind a bus
like a street cat with a bin.
Say we caught him.
Say we burned his clothes
by the mountains and the sea.
Say we broke each other
relentlessly. My brother
lay under a truck for hours
only for seven years in
a tent. Tents like these
make no difference.
Difference is what we encounter
at the tree where apathies meet.
I want more than my father's sorrow.
I am dissatisfied with the life
that is borrowed.
Say we sat under the tree
and watched the torchlights
sweep the streets of Bethlehem.
Say we wept again.
Say we didn't stop weeping,
this game of trying
to grieve our friends.

COLONIAL APOLOGIST

Squall beneath the water: beyond
the horizon, where stirrings take root.

Diving into the depths of adivinity,
I write myself into a meaningful oblivion:

on fire, underwater, soundless,
the rattling of a snare drum.

I want to make my cacophonies legible:
this is how to stop undoing my own defensives.

And then you first resurface, the beginnings
of apology arrested halfway out of your throat,

barracuda writhing, half-torso out of your mouth
thrashing its tail, and it triangulates its body, burrowing

into the waves in twisting fins. Our *Scheherazade*:
all the while you are forming an oceanic forgiveness

before words can come out of the mouth.
When do we learn to say we are sorry

when we know that we are right?
I swim until I forget that I am right.

Sharks swim until they forget that they are sharks.
Now we both live in mutual apology.

Remember how the throat arrests the sound of fury,
how the voice catches, and we are inconsolable.

BATH TOWEL SITS AT THE INTERSECTION OF TWO CHAIRS

Jorie Graham looks for an image, a line & an ear. Neither of us have even one of these. Chiara says her problem is writing too much meta-poetry & my problem is taking myself too seriously. It's only as she says this that I realise why I've been struggling with showers: it is difficult to retrieve a landmark when I will not be orderly again for days & the days are like minefields & the minefields trophies. The intimacy of this vexes me like a bad simile. We laugh like we're laughing drily, we promise to be less pretentious & read more Glück (for sparseness, or proximity).

AFTER ME

The chords for "Sunday Candy" and "Wait for the Moment" are the same. My most tender realisations bloom in the middle of things. The mountains are catching the mist, and all my friends are being whipped into shape by career civil servants who despise Naomi Osaka. How else to explain the kid then? I want to ask. I am only sure of consequent unsafety. Mental health is false even to the educated middle class in this small town, which I suppose is also why it took us so many years to say the word "depression".

WHAT IS MASCULINITY BUT ADOLESCENCE WITHOUT END?

Violent men make sense to me.
Elm trees burst with leaves &
rustle with eulogies for those
riven despite themselves.

Despite themselves the leaves
are metaphors for killing.
Unsubtle branches muscular
like riflemen & their arms.

Still, The Boys rap The Roots
at parties. Still, the trunk is ringed
with the marching of time, holding
the weight of seized-up bodies.
The steadfastness of men takes
different forms: banning girls from
playground slides, quoting Cixous,
breaking all that they cannot have.

GRACE

On the day my mother forgives me, the watermelons in NTUC are on offer. I remember to drum the green bodies and listen for echoes, choose one that seems better only because he is mine. We stare at each other in silence on the way home, my belonging sitting upright in my lap. His black stripes remind me of a tiger, but then so does everything else. In the dream where it happens, the tigers are lying on their sides in the sun; when we stop in front of them, one gets up and paces in front like a tensile bodyguard. It might have been a zoo, or a forest, or a documentary, I am no longer sure if this is a memory from my youth or a story that I had read. When the jam-break happens, there is surprise like it comes from outside of me. All of a sudden the bus uncle is shouting, and there is pink flesh flooding the floor of the bus; all of a sudden, my heart is filled with a brutal loving.

FARM MART

Two children, one Boston baseball cap.
Twice we call out, *ke yi wei ma*.
Speak English, Papa says,
pull up your socks.

Together we roll grass into kebeh,
nibbles texturing offering
in palms outstretched as fronds.
Mama scoops a brother up,
offers him like a burnt sacrifice,
contours half-creolised mouth-shapes
into a question mark.

The sunset soon.
Quietly we come, and quietly we will go.
The italics are not translation.

The next day I read the word 'evanescent'
in a novel, mispronounce it,
learn to roll the 's' and 'c' together,
in quick breath.

MILES

That's really—she stops. Nam Le's words are floating just beyond my eyeline: she looked like an actress who looked like my girlfriend.

Stop biting your nails, she says instead, a small mercy and the final blow. Sorry, I say, and stop biting my nails.

The world of my room feels muscular and caged. There is a pause, and we both look away from the screen. Maybe, I try, I was looking for some solidarity. My words are lame and small and evanescent even to me. We are two months away from the end—a fact we didn't know yet but had known for some time.

Thank god you're not like that anymore, she says. Yeah, I say, biting my nails. Thank god.

ANDREW KIRKROSE DEVADASON

INTERLOPER SAYS

Rabbits taw and nun more.
I slept away my sac and yew.
I have had enough of theogony.

Meatstaple me, kyría, and leave
the maul out to dry. Eye had no answer.
Soften, only soften the fole.

Roe star elide, uncouth the ante.
PUNISHMENT, unfaltering.
behoove.behoove.behooves.

behoove.behoove.behoove.
I found the name in a graveyard.
It still does not belong to you.

Fair grounds move all night.
I don't even believe in gourds.

GLASS VASE CELLO CASE

For the song by Tattle Tale

I cannot whistle over the rim of a bottle, which is why
I play the drums and not the flute. I have never had a dream
in which my body is made of melting sand
but maybe I should start. I dream in ooze and rot
and acid. Girlmeat turned boymeat turned wound. Fill me
with star and paper, or spit and ash, or flower and more dust.
I don't really care what. I told you I like being filled up. Like it
when you hit me. It's the fear of not being able to handle it, the relief of discovering
I can. Take it, I mean.
Nothing so exquisite as raised fist
and knowing I'm worth the effort of impact.
The winter I turned thirteen, I thought I was a lesbian.
So I listened to Tegan and Sara, and sat through
every episode of *The L Word*, just to be safe. Cultural immersion
is important. I can't hold my breath in water. Can't stand
the feeling of liquid on my eyes. I've watched *But I'm
a Cheerleader* with every romantic partner I've had.
Lying in bed, holding hands. I've watched it at least
ten times. It feels like coming home, but good.
I could have been a good lesbian. I've read the Sappho
(trans. Carson 2003). But the violets died in my lap.
There's no space for cellos in the percussion/woodwind binary
and frankly there's nothing a cello can do that a bass and a viola
can't. But bassi and viole aren't as sexy as sobs.
What's so good about sounding human? I've held
hands with enough humans to know
it's nothing new.
Queer curation is queer creation, I say, about to watch
the same movie for the fifteenth time. This is barely a joke.
Do you ever read so hard into a text it feels like you're the one
writing it?

PREPARATION FOR / CLEANSING THE BLOOD

For Warman's Bottles Field Guide *by Michael Polak*

Nothing grows but Naptha, wild cherry
in the junkyard where boys break bottles
for the marbles held inside. You learn to drink tar
from the King of Pain herself, sheared lip
pressed to rolled lip pressed to bent neck
with finger grooves bruised in back. Butterfly bolts
suckle bubble pack, whiskey turning bitter as the sky
flips stations. Beneath the table, a bellows breathes
dust and empty changes hands. You were taught
the value of a proper closure. All else is slow drip.
Not To / Be Sold whistles over melon ribs, sloped collars,
the wide mouths of colourless cathedrals.

EXCERPT FROM "THE SPARE PARTS CYCLE"

With thanks to Jack Xi

vi. conditional clauses

if the mirror is a bowl for the soul
if the soul is something like saliva
if everyone else can spit God from
     between their shining teeth

if your teeth are in your way again
if there is no way to overcome teeth
if my teeth scrape against your skin
     just the way he used to like it

if I look in the mirror and see nothing
if I look in the mirror and see myself
if I don't look in the mirror anymore
     telling myself it will be empty

if these eyes are the opening window
if this breeze hails the next monsoon
if that frangipani tree is only a tree and
     no one is wearing her perfume

(if a boy in the skin of a girl sits there)
(if his eyes open to the falling leaves)
(if a nonhuman in the skin of a human
     sits there with him and smiles)

if I called my lovers over the threshold
if I called my lovers over telephone wire
if I called them lovers and they believed
     I had a heart and it could beat

if love is you looking through windows
if love is you spitting goldenrod spit
if love is you covering the mirror so
    as to shield the shining sun

(if a boy molts on the bathroom floor)
(if the boy counts every shred of skin)
(if the boy denies it three times and
    never once hears a rooster)

if I have no blood to feel running cold
if I have no heart to feel icing over
if I have no reflection to see growing
    older than those I left behind

if there are too many stars to count
if there is only wide, illiberal sky
if there is nothing written up there
    you consider worth reading

(if a boy cracks his own ribs apart)
(if he lies in the dark and counts)
(if he watches his own open heart
    in someone else's hands)

if she asked me if I had finished
if she herself had no plans to finish
if all she felt was his teeth and not
    my thirstfilled open mouth

if the stakes are too high this time
if my parents sharpen their stakes
if they never put away their blessed
    medallions, my old medals

if I say the word love enough times
if I say the mirror won't be empty
if I say the window is open and don't
     count the closed doorways

if it was really an accident this time
if they never needed that exorcist
if there's no body to find because
     I'm still here, goddammit

if there is room for me on this earth
if there is room for me in this body
if there is room where my heart is
     for things that hearts hold

if my ribs stay intact just this once
if I am no longer holding their cage
if I look in the mirror and no longer
     flinch at what looks back

(if a boy puts on the skin of a poet)
(if a boy puts on another poet's skin)
(if a boy puts down a condition and
     then another and another and
          another and an other)

TRUTH CONDITIONS

$((((\neg G \cdot \neg P) \cdot (((S \rightarrow B) \lor (\neg Y \cdot R)) \lor ((A \cdot H) \cdot (E \rightarrow C)))) \lor ((K \cdot (\neg U \cdot W)) \cdot (\neg M \rightarrow T))) \rightarrow (((((((I \cdot M) \cdot \neg J) \cdot (Y \cdot \neg E)) \lor D) \lor ((L \cdot \neg Z) \cdot M)) \lor ((P \cdot (\neg X \cdot V)) \cdot \neg R)) \cdot ((((T \rightarrow Q) \cdot U) \rightarrow (F \cdot \neg O)) \rightarrow (H \rightarrow \neg N))))$

A: Every photo in the family album is of someone who is not me.
B: My name is bubbling over on the stovetop of our domesticity.
C: Even a scared crow knows what's coming.
D: I trace my lineage on the future axis.
E: A shot rings out.
F: I skim what I need off the froth of my mistakes.
G: Grandma is alive.
H: Hell is a mirror that does not recognise your face.
I: I introduce myself as myself.
J: No one takes me seriously.
K: I flip through Eve Kosofsky Sedgwick's *Epistemology of the Closet*.
L: I hold your hand.
M: My heartbeat is steady.
N: I am there.
O: Guilt digs a pit right through me.
P: The pastor is watching.
Q: I have gone through every letter of the alphabet to find my name.
R: Someone at the sink sneers.
S: The sunshine has become too much for me to bear.
T: I put the book down.
U: I understand everything as if for the first time.
V: I wash my hands at the soup kitchen.
W: The words go in one eye and out the other.
X: I take off our wedding ring.
Y: I walk into the correct bathroom.
Z: I make sure the door is closed.

THIS BLENDER GRINDS THE MEAT

*For "We visited a meat-processing factory to find out
exactly how McDonald's hamburgers are made"
by Lisa Boerop and Qayyah Moynihan,* Business Insider Nederland

i.

they disappear my number
into blue plastic bags, then
boxes. a few are always
tested but never the ones
I want. within hours, the
slaughterhouse. the farm.
die in your country of origin
for a shorter way to go.

ii.

Hungry at a rate of seventy-five a second, I persisted
fourteen ears, took it like a welcome call
to concern, my worry exponent
on another horizon.

iii.

metalbugleg knows
my illness.
checks meat ensuring there are
no bones.
nothing is allowed to go loose
in this
factory. plastic pens will not go
unnoticed.
even the reception area smells
of beef.
raincoat me, dandy. forklift me
utterly.
not one cadaver but
dozens.

iv.

The microbes that cause rotting are much
like myself in that what we need
to survive we want
to fall apart.

SEED

For Chikako Yamashiro's Mud man

some seed fell into rich soil/others fell on sunburnt shoulders/will you spill your seed on my shoulder/if i ask nicely?

if i bury a seed/if i bury the lede/if i bury myself/what will grow?

what is there to show for this terroir but seed/what is there to show for this terror but seed/who has seen enough of the terror to know/what the terroir has yet to show?

if this is still my war/then i think it's terribly unfair that i'm still the only one in uniform/will you paint my eyelids with sleep/when we've all run out of seeds?

your balancing point against/my pressure points gave/me a terrible headache/so why am I still singing?

if you swallowed my seed because i asked/if i swallowed your seed before you asked/which of us will come out of it smelling/like roses and just who will be singing?

some seed fell off a cliff and/into the boundless ocean where/no one sings anymore so/why do i keep diving in?

if i'm drowning in song and/you're drowning in poems/should i still be writing this/from beneath sea foam?

some seed fell from the sky then/climbed its way back/i don't think my hands know how to grasp any more/why is there nothing but air at my back?

if i can't take flight because/my wings took flight without/the proper precautions then/when will they grow back?

some seed fell on me/i don't think it was yours/i think i'm growing into something new/do i have any choice but to sing?

if i can't stop singing/if i can't stop sinking/if there is seed in the sky and the sea and the soil/what does that make of the seed growing in me?

IN ENDLESS ITERATION

". . . Adam and Adam's answer in the forest . . ."—*"Cape Hatteras"*, Hart Crane

always a rib	stirring
feminine	or raw
or iridescent	it is best
treated as if	to be borne
empty handed	over time
trusted	as if heavy
with the wound	of late
of a body in delay	cut through
weighed down	by trust
too long	with nothing to show
all is to be borne	in retreat
the best meat is	iridescent
still raw, still	feminine
stirring	but always a rib

SEVENTEEN

After Bend It Like Beckham

This isn't about sex, obviously, you holding your covers to your neck to hide the bra you aren't wearing, me standing and looking down at you and you looking up at me and our eyes not meeting. I'm seventeen and you're seventeen and we're just two named female characters having a conversation with each other about love, only it's about some guy named Joe who was probably written in at the last minute after a focus group or a screen-test or some kind of meeting with a bunch of rich dudes in suits. There's no Mother Bechdel in the wings or the sky or anywhere, just us and the lighter in my pocket that I said I wouldn't take out of the kitchen cause I'd fiddle with it but I took it with me today and I'm fiddling with it and I've had fire on my fingertips twice today already. Looks like it's going to be a third time because now you're telling me I've *really hurt you*, like I didn't know that already, like there isn't some goddamn guy in this room with us, watching us talk, who isn't a God like this isn't about sex, who isn't cartoonist-creator-breaker-of-fourth-walls. Like this isn't all about the male gaze or some other kind of homophone. Should have saved the fire for burning the chapatis, for melting candle wax while some voice that isn't yours or mine or anyone's says *that's a sex thing you know* and some other voice says *everything's a sex thing if you try hard enough* and some third thing says *everything's a God if you try hard enough* but maybe it's not you, it's me, or it's him (isn't it always?) or maybe it's no one. Maybe I'm as much no one as the look on your face is saying, or maybe you do want me here as much as the look on your face is saying, or maybe you do want me dead as much as the look on your face is saying, my fingertips scorched red to match my thighs. Maybe that's what would have happened in the version where it was really just us in this room, the version where you hang the rope up from the hook in your closet, the version where I take down all my posters and the easy way out, the one where you're on your bed and I'm standing here and our eyes do meet. But that's not what this is, so of course I won't die. I'm seventeen and you're seventeen and we're just two named female characters having a conversation with each other about love, only it's about some guy here in the room with us now.

WHY ARE YOU STILL LYING AT THE WEIGHING OF THE HEART?

i.

The unclarity of water.
The slow tremble of colour through that medium.

Spreading underground
from what is buried and knows it. The project of wiring

a partial skeleton to any
fixed form. The solder of impurity in a body

with no breakers. The swirling
descent of a beetle who trades her green wings

for death. The solvent
of suggested answer. By dye in water, did you mean

to drown? The bargainer's sign
reading *order only what you can finish*. The light

strobing at the right speed.
Or so they hope. The phone ringing haematoma. Hands

shaking through a controlled pour.
Incomplete. The desire path bisecting cemetery and statuary.

ii.

Boy as state of hunger. Not-boy as state of meat.

iii.

I want to strip the body
of its materiality, this tunnel

I cannot see my way through.
I mean this body, this figure absent

from the figuration of my life.
I mean this shape that escapes

the lens lest I lose momentum
in my skimming-stone self.

I mean my meat and blood
and bone. To be grounded

is the wrong kind of sentence.
I am riddled with loss, every experience

filtered through a body that I have
or a body I do not, at least one

of two kinds of wound. Corpus
and still-haunted corpse.

iv.

sea me now. no more sex for me. i want to be
unsexed. want to breathe again. give me
green pastures, shining in negative. paint me
read, daddy. i want it all to end in a tree
rotten solid with stars. or i meant scars.
nothing finishes when you mean it to.
unroot me, god, or some other holy other.
i am singing this song alone.

v.

I opened a box. Searched
for Not Available and other locations.
The oldest question I knew.

How fruit grows
drinking interference
of air.

They stripped the road in layers, ten thousand
leaves cleaner than
ragged nails can peel.

I hear more
clearly when the light
is on.

It was
red meat underneath, or
I was hungry.

SYMPATHETIC RESONANCE

For Paul Baker's Fabulosa! *and the Sisters of Perpetual Indulgence*

Vada that quivering lucoddy set
astir with your Gloria's polari.
Her dowry dally voche. Duckie,
all your mother wants is a bona
bijou hearing cheat, attuned to
the chant of her own sweet
thumping cheat. Cackle to her
otterly, dearie. Nanti dander.
Mary has your number. Sweet
strillers will set the curtains
to rattle, yes, in your lattie
and of all those in the life.
Let it be so, sister. Let us be so.

MARYLYN TAN

DADDY ISSUES

so they're putting out an edition for SG50:
shades of red—

last night, I was suspended
from the ceiling by a rope harness,
made to candlewax
lyrical about the progress
our nation has made.
sir told me our safeword could be
paternalism—no—censorship—no—*welfare*.

thank you sir may I please have another
thank you sir may I please have another
look at all you've accomplished,
all your foreskinned foresight

don't you know the judicial caning penalty
is just teaching you to clench
your buttocks in fear

when grey berets
gang up on you at crowded
intersections
demanding
where's your passport? and what's in
your backpack?—
but that's only for your own good.

so I sucked it up like I was already used to enemas,
allowed Sir to plug his indoctrination
into my ass
an anal plug shaped
like a remote control
was told to hold
it—hold
it—
hold—

if you work hard enough maybe you'll earn the right
to sleep
in a bed tonight
a BTO
married life
housing rights
safety from racial profiles
political exiles
who's a good girl?

who's
a
good girl?

sir I can't hold it anymore.
I think all my indignation
is leaking out.

so they told me to be quiet
dribble my anger into
the GDP squatting over a bucket
labelled worker productivity
straining to boost the economy

sir controls access to basic commodity
just so you won't be lazy.
maybe if you satisfy sir tonight
you'll be allowed clean water
and food and air.

you're just a useless little slut
for being spoon fed basic necessities,

aren't you?

but if you don't like it then why don't you
just live in some other dungeon.
don't you know compared to other slaves

you're already very spoilt?
don't you need your strong, first-world dom
to protect you against the big bad
terrorism slash Marxism slash civil unrest slash alternative lifestyles?

do you want to be one of those slaves
whose heads are shaved?
don't you know conscription
is just another humiliation,
because if we bond over dick jokes we might forget
we   bend over in service
to the nation

might forget
our testes
are in someone else's fist.

what do you mean, is this blindfold necessary?
it's not like you see anything
I don't want you to see
on the internet
unless it's a falsehood
that I've personally fact-checked

why don't you bring me back into office
so you can crawl back between my legs
and tell me how much you like it under my desk.

Daddy's happy that you're happy
I mean it makes you happy daddy's happy
I mean, daddy's happy that
you're happy that he's happy
I mean if you're not happy
we can talk about it

but first put on this ball gag

A WET CRIMSON BUSHEL OF PEARS

stay me with flagons, comfort me with apples:
for I am sick of love.
—Song of Solomon, 2:5 KJV

perhaps scatter the scarred breadcrumbs   far and few
between and   the trail will seem shorter   every day
is a desert   waylaid in   the back of my throat
prickly-pear me into sustenance   this body is betrayal
look at these protesting joints   my one weeping eye   these
allergies   swelling my voice shut
I think often   about taking a long trek
on short notice   maybe   I wouldn't like the
sand much but I'd find it   easier to be, there
unhampered the moon unhinged the coyotes all
those wayward symbols of   death   buzzards not
so easy   made corporeal   gifts given   short shrift
when   we get everything we want   which is now
the first thing   embroiled in happenstance   and
the brilliance of firelight   stoking menace
find me a perfect stone   upon which to rest my head
no other crutch   smooth just as wisdom is a wine
milky battered   and perhaps   sheltering a serpent
we come here to bleach our bones in unerring light
such that   everything crumbles   returned to me
various heaving heavinesses   spilt salt across   a dark stain spreads
under the single-minded glaring eye of horus
I don't dare bring my feeble doubts   no longer
the pacing   only the being
                                still   a feat

Excerpted from THE OSCAR ROSARY, *forthcoming from Gutslut Press.*

THE OSCAR ROSARY

is a combination
of vocal and mental prayer
on the mysteries of our redemption
it is composed of
the LITANY OF OUR OSCAR, the LITANIES OF QUESTIONING,
and an
APOLOGY (TRUTH),
ending with the FAG FEMME UP EJACULATION

A PIOUS CUSTOM:
A Pious custom assigns the different Apologies to different days of the week, as follows:
READ EVERY APOLOGY THAT APPLIES ON THE DAY OF THE WEEK IN WHICH YOU ARE PERFORMING DEVOTION, OR EXISTING.
THE JOYFUL (GAY) APOLOGIES
THE SORROWFUL (BYE) APOLOGIES
THE GLORIOUS (LOL SIENTO) APOLOGIES

THE DEDICATION

To be recited at the beginning of the Rosary.

Celebrant The love / that dare not speak its name / had not protected / him.
All Your silence / will not protect you.[1]

The participants are arranged in a semi-circle around the celebrant. The room is lit with sixteen candles so that each and every face is visible, but an atmosphere of semi-anonymity is preserved. While performing, eye contact with the participants is mandatory as far as possible, especially while the celebrant is speaking. Ensure there is an empty chair within the seating area. The celebrant may sit on this chair at any time but has to ask for permission from participants. The participants may be composed of as large or as small a number as is necessary to elicit discomfort.

---

[1] "The love that dare not speak its name." Lord Alfred Douglas, Oscar Wilde's lover, "Two Loves" "My silences had not protected me. Your silence will not protect you," Audre Lorde, *The Cancer Journals*

LITANY OF OUR OSCAR AS TRAGIC GAY ICON

To be read aloud by the celebrant. The participants respond with the words in italics. In the event of audience members not possessing THE OSCAR ROSARY, *alternative responses are to respond in any audible way they deem appropriate.*

Celebrant	**All**
Oscar as tragic gay icon	*we see you*
Oscar as foppish flamboyant dandy aesthete	*we see you*
Oscar as victim of blackmail	*we see you*
Oscar as victim of neglect	*we see you*
Oscar as victim through invisibility	*we see you*
Oscar as victim of inert unattended bisexuality	*we see you*
Oscar as estranged father	*we see you*
Oscar as body-negative misogynist	*we see you*
Oscar as convicted of offence against the Crown	*we see you*
Oscar as the only blot on one's tutelage	*we see you*
Oscar as failed hedonist	*we see you*
Oscar as the happy prince	*we see you*
Oscar as starving artist	*we see you*
Oscar as disease-ridden corpse	*we see you*
Oscar as a portrait of malaise	*we see you*
Oscar as dying destitute	*we see you*
Oscar as tombstone	*we see you*
Oscar as the strange male on the corner of a street	*we know you*
Oscar as a homely woman	*we know you*
Oscar as mansplainer	*we know you*
Oscar as repeating your opinion and receiving the credit for it	*we know you*
Oscar as a recipient of bullying	*we know you*
Oscar as your mother	*we know you*
Oscar as my mother	*we know you*
Oscar as the deaconness serving a Black Mass of the Anglican Order	*we know you*
Oscar as Saint Sebastian	*we know you*
Oscar as Jesus	*we know you*

Oscar as a sex object   *we made you*
Oscar as a bedside glazed ceramic dildo in aluminum trashcan   *we made you*
Oscar as an apron stain   *we made you*
Oscar as the whet blade   on the lovelorn side chopping
           block hands flecked like
                      doves sprinkled red   *we made you*
Oscar as a lone tomato   *we made you*
Oscar as a Mitsubishi rice rocket
     that is
        an Asian motorcycle *zhng'd up ah beng* style   *we made you*
Oscar as rickshaw wheel   *we made you*
Oscar as third wheel   *we made you*
Oscar as the swallow on the statue's shoulder   *we made you*
Oscar as the swallow of the cum load   *we made you*
Oscar as the crocodilian godhead
     weighing your feckless heart
           against a puffin feather   *we made you*

Oscar as pleasure in disagreeing with you   *we seek you*
Oscar as bitterly disappointed   *we seek you*
Oscar as intimidating   *we seek you*
Oscar as transcendent   *we seek you*
Oscar as unflappable   *we seek you*
Oscar as unfuckable with   *we seek you*
Oscar as unfuckable   *we seek you*

All   Deliver us always from that from which you could not save yourself, and pray for us like they prayed for you.

The Celebrant extinguishes Candle 1.

Excerpted from THE OSCAR ROSARY, THE THIRD AND FINAL GLORIOUS APOLOGY, *forthcoming from Gutslut Press.*

THIS IS HOW TO SLAUGHTER A BIRD YOU OBTAIN FROM THE MARKET

suffering is one long moment.
this is how you slaughter a chicken
you have carefully selected
purchased for your family
at the wet market.

already you are familiar with the wings,
the four-limbed job,
your hair falling over
in the frantic flutter thrumming
like an amputee cockroach.

take the glaring eyes and mismatched throat. the thorn
will edge its way into your secret place. yours is
the knowledge of the close-cropped, stippled skin,
a drum outstretched, like grasping the tip of one's member
with forefinger and thumb, pulled tight. three days sat
puddled in three fluids. brow-water, heart's-blood,
cock-spend pearly as sea foam.

be watchful that your feathered foul
does not do that.

pluck the throat bare
in nimble jerking movement.
the gibbering shudder
in your flat-footed attempt
with the sawing motion.

be watchful of
opening the neck
in that fashion.

one might
sustain stains.

this part is swiftest.
time does not spurt forth
crass and wanton,
but drips in a runny stream,
slow pulsing flow.

let no nightingale pass
between your lips / they, palming,
squirm between your thighs
two clamped pillars of turkey breast alabaster

tuck / the drained head / underwing
so they leap blind, a folded stutter
wrung almost
to completion.

all claws are beautiful
but claws enfeebled
are unbearable.

a wrist working
its slow witch way
through that place
where it fits

remember the stretch sounding
at the water-leak, the emptying slit,
made to sag gagging wider
to better abet pleasure.

after the fowl is collapsed and
huddled, corner-wise, one prepares
the boiling water. questions
how long a moment lasts, a
sip of time. three times a dip,
lightly boiled. then to strip
the remaining feathers.

QUEER FILTH INFERNAL

After Dante Alighieri's Inferno

unbelievable, unceasing,
irresistible, unignorable,
in these negatives I only
ghost my hands over
the unknowable shape
of what you are.

love last, love lost;
in this blatant mirage
only one can speak
figures you'd come
for me anyway my
gothic poet laureate
candescent ex fucking your
unctuous glossy fingers

into my parting desert dune
reading murder blackfeather poetry
in this circle dirty is a city
and my fey words reach you
before running in labyrinthine
thicknesses. a wailing, a
good time, she who is called

Incontinence slavering over
us who've made our vows
and burn them in the ash.

my love, sodom, widen
each pouting sphincter
of my hidden wisdom
grant the caplet teeth
my salvation with your
crown of mud and suckling
gift. your godhead, torn
asunder,

a defiant *kiap*ping of
my thighs, between your
thighs. came down
to the river styx and all
we saw was a wedding
boat, charon's nickel tongue
another rusted openmouth
kiss, bleeding me out

your achilles heel I have
grasped naked o never
let us be those inheriting

the yoke of those who
never lived and can
never die

CURSING THE FIG TREE: THE HOLY PREPUCE & OTHER DELICIOUS RECIPES

1. *Crying and with compassion,*
    she began to think about

    the foreskin of Christ,
    where it may be located
    [after the Resurrection].

    And behold,
    soon she felt
    with the greatest sweetness
    on her tongue
    a little piece of skin alike
    the skin in an egg,

    which she swallowed.[1]

---

[1] Wiethaus, Ulrike (2002). *Agnes Blannbekin, Viennese Beguine: Life and Revelations.*

2. they call it fasting but time passes so slow   tasty christ.   pasty
curly-haired blue-eyed middle-eastern christ. women saints pickled in shrine sin gorge us swole rolling eyes animals in tongues of flame   panty cost   nailed to the cross nailed on the bed   never find anyone else who burns so easy
      joan of arc was made of flesh   joan of arc was maid of orleans
        we only barbecue the saints that mean the most to us

turn the other cheek so fast
you get self-flagellating whiplash   kyrie e e ele e e i son   lord have mercy
    ✜ALCHEMICAL SYMBOL FOR VINEGAR—THE JERUSALEM CROSS—beat me gently with a hyssop stick—lift me to the martyred lips—the guilt an art form—

    the knees a penance—

    the pursed lips a furrowed heave   church organ donors hollow within gutted   indelible inedible incredible liturgical litany ritual rutting serpent gloaming egg gut archly theological venial veal transgressions being

    WITH THE ASCENSION OF JESUS, ALL OF HIS BODY PARTS—
EVEN THOSE NO LONGER ATTACHED—ASCENDED WITH HIM

    THE FORESKIN OF CHRIST WAS TRANSFORMED
        INTO THE RINGS
            OF SATURN[2]

---

[2] Fabricius, Johann Albert (1728). *Bibliotheca Graeca (Vol. 14)* (in Latin). Hamburg. p. 17. *Adhuc ineditis praefixus Astericus.* Unpublished work.

3. *THIS IS MY BODY*

concept: a confessional box with a red light on / like an invitation / or a warning
concept: jesus as a teenaged girl. this is my body. this is my blood

in the beginning
the word was made flesh

jesus, taught the shame of a
sinful body, of a receptacle-like body, a true
vessel of christ. jesus being taught to keep his
legs closed

turns out
the chalice of the holy grail
is a menstrual cup

jesus christ
& the silicone goblet of fluids
jesus not being able to enter
the very temple where he preaches

jesus' mom telling him to
   GET RID OF THE BLOOD
with bared teeth &
barely-concealed disgust

jesus' schoolmates chanting
   PLUG IT UP, PLUG IT UP
in the girls' bathroom

throwing tampons at jesus
convinced they would fit
in the holes / in his hands & feet

the stigma of the stigmata
jesus doesn't have access to:
   the internet/ the feminine mystique/   the bleeding as power
     all he knows is potency / transmuted into poison

fire /
      into filth
      the same day jesus learnt to cover his shame
      he figured out the Holy Prepuce of Christ
      meant jesus' foreskin

      the saviour's / private areas
                    popularised / by the uncanonised
                            Agnes Blannbekin's / holy visions
                    enthusiastically transcribed
      by her confessor
                    a monk fascinated with
                        the body of christ
jesus pulls his robes a little tighter
doesn't want to be one of *those* prophets
at the last supper / subsisting on celery & water
this is my body   this is
my blood. tonight we dine
but will throw it back up / roman catholic
                        vomitorium

because you always see a jacked christ but you never see a fat christ / the dadbod of christ /
the kate moss waif-like figure of christ / perpendicular stick thin christ

            why were the faithful crying / at the eucharistic feast? because christ had been
a way fer so long   why were the faithful hungry at the eucharistic feast? A
LITTLE PIECE OF SKIN ALIKE THE SKIN IN AN EGG
     communing in communion calorie count

it's one drink of vinegar / it's one piece of eggskin
     it's one apple
          for chrissakes

                            EAT ME
in the beginning
the word was made flesh
& some people say / that word was yes

this is my body, for public consumption
this is my body, salvation of swarming crowds

jesus has lost count of how many times
his ass has been stroked surreptitious   back of the hand
by the faceless faithful
              it's called backpalming because the fronts of your palms are pressed together
in penance

WHO   TOUCHED ME

jesus said, (Luke 8:45)

who   touched me
again

jesus finds walking on water easier
than walking home alone at night
jesus walks with nails /clenched between his knuckles
if he didn't want to be crucified
he shouldn't have manifested in human form
if he didn't want us to tear it
he shouldn't have worn a one-piece seamless garment
he shouldn't have let the holy spirit in him
doesn't he know how many people
the holy spirit's been inside of?

maybe jesus still awakes dislodged some nights
the memory of thorns crowding his temples
& the only way he survives is by resurrecting the incident
but this time he controls / who flagellates him
whiplash trauma / requires exercise to heal /

jesus' safe space

is a tomb hewn in rock
a safeword like a great stone
rolling across his tongue
amen / amen / amen
amen /

amen

they nailed him to the cross with his legs closed
like a good girl /
like a good girl
jesus

crying silently in the garden of gethsemane
so as not to wake the others
allowing judas to kiss him / rather than resist him

jesus / still can be a Cool Girl if he wants

this is my body / take it & eat it
& never
ever
mention the blood

4. *In 1900, the Roman Catholic church ruled that anyone thenceforward writing or speaking of the Holy Prepuce would be excommunicated.*[3]

---

[3] Farley, David (2006). "Fore Shame." Slate.com.

TAGGED 'SINGAPORE': A SELECTION OF TITLES FOUND ACROSS *XHAMSTER*, *XNXX*, *XVIDEOS*, AND *PORNHUB*

(Content warnings: porn, possible non-consensual sharing, racialised content)

                Cum pours out of Chinese Lin
     sg buttcheek xmm
         BellyWJ Blinded BJ
     the Fucking Sound ~ #1
     singapore uppant
Arsenal Blow Job
           triple shoejob on one cock

AsianSexPorno.com - Asian girl get hoot
     Big tits malaysian indian from Singapore 1
     Hot Chinese pussy get the long White
         MELAYU SOLO
             indian aunty 720p
     Chinese hottie in Singapore
Hotel tourist with maley

You can fuck me but you can't cum inside of me   Silky Asshole In Sweaty Singapore
     Savvy from Signapore fingering in her parental house   Rectal Buggerations With Creamy Singapore BabeSlant Eyed
         We missed the Singapore Grand Prix for this?!!

Super Slim Singapore Babe Shouts For Sex   SG amateur sex video leaked by his boyfriend   singapore chinatown waxing service
     look at my cum singapore
         I love singapore

             Singapore Girl want bf to WANK
             singapore SYT girl upblouse
                 Singapore Ah Lian fuck   Singapore Chinese Sweet

Young Thing   Singapore Sinner Fucked For Cash   Singapore random
     Singapore prison cane - Double judicial   Singapore Gong Cha Girl
    Singapore Sengkang Sluts
Singapore Accountant Regina

         nice face
             The real outdoor fun

       She worked her way from the street to
       the bar where she proffered her rectum
       to tourists on vacation. Right there in
       the bar, she would get buggered up the
       shitter, with a vibrator stuffed up her
       cunt

Singapore impatient
    sg ass show
       singapore ladies shopping without wearing bra
           shiok shiok singapore
        shaky shaky boobs singapore
               suck dick in the morning chicken dinner
                     faster la please

HAMID ROSLAN

THE SHAPE OF A BODY UNCERTAIN

I.

        Once, it was written that there was a man who slipped onto a ship and sailed off the edge.　　　When the monsoon lash returned him, the man failed to feel the sticky that pressed.　　　The man could not eat the cooked.　　　The man spoke to silence.　　　And of the most, the man was blind to she with the heaven-scented feet.　　　It was written that she cursed the man to stone in the tropics, iced her son who slipped,

ibarat kacang, kaleidoscoping, (Pihak
∓ 5.67 calories), irgendwo auf der Welt,

Fries-Frau, frequently identifying as Melayu,
but at one point when Judith says
her house is slick

describes herself as Arab,
"orang Melayu malas
bukan macam orang Arab",

ibarat die Frau am das Visayanischen
Ufer spreche Jerman und Englisch mit Deutsch
Accent aber Haben Sie Malaischen Familienname?

isch
isch
isch

ibarat
a revol-
         -vol
Tür

ibarat
yes,
yes:

All she said when she called was:
She is no more.
She is no more.

The sun was gone.
And who knows what I was at the time.
She told me once

that if one goes the way She went,
in the pursuit of knowledge,
then one will arrive at the Gate

without question. Given the fact
we are to say *And it is we who are His*
and to Him are we returned we are demanded

demanded to sink the body and weep
only to dampen the top
but all I heard was Come.

Please. Can you please come?

But what hewed the body while it was out there?
      It was written that boys were found in sliced peaches, but it was also written that women sprang from skulls.
In this case shall we then say the son began as cut fruit browning in a fridge?
Was it that the relentless decay of the tropics scattered the son, now stone?
     And was his return the end of a recognised starving, in anticipation for what was to come?

We are legislation
worked out to tighten the loosening
here and elsewhere.

How did anyone expect a woman
to search the papers and place
her mother's body

into the line? Is that relevant
it was said, but it was also said
and over you are those who bear witness,

the noble, and the recording,
they know every deed.
It was recited before it was written.

A Chinese account says
they make rafts of trees bound together,
and build houses on the water,

and if fire was detected
each owner cuts the cables,
floats away and then ties up elsewhere,

far from the conflagration.
So it is with water and the stone,
with policy and the bonsai,

with luck and the one-dollar talisman,
with island and the mush slyline,
with bite and the leash against the living.

So she took her son now stone home, the slip shipped again.

      At every meal she made him eat the melange only the tropics could provide.

      She tried exacting forgiveness but all passed the scrape.

      Granite flinched from the shine. The laundry stooped to look.

      What else could she do?

      Padanya yang penjaga patung batu, ruang dapur menjadi perkakas bagikan seseorang memiliki alam.

```
                                        Anak aku
drip-attrition
                                        Anak aku
      leaky sink
                                        Anak aku
scry
                      So she took her son now
Anak aku              stone home, the slip
       occlusion  of  a   shipped again.          chain of events
                              At every me-
Anak aku              al she made him eat the
is    as     quickly  melange only the tropics   as
                      could provide.
Anak aku                      She tried ex-
    forgets           acting forgiveness but all
                      passed the scrape.
Anak aku                      Granite
        will hurt     flinched from the shine.   with enough
                      The laundry stooped to
Anak aku              look.
     will be little use for a   What else could she   sentence
                      do?
Anak aku              Padanya yang penjaga
will walk into dangled  patung batu, ruang dapur   modifier
                      menjadi perkakas bagikan
                      seseorang memiliki alam.
Anak aku
will judge how                  far
                                        Anak aku
will carry       the metre without pause.
```

The moments I spent in and out of sleep,

watching Her shrouded, hunched over herself, profuse in speech

to He who listened. I do not know what Her genuflection meant.

Let us say that She has done this in all the days that I remember Her

occupying, without question, incessantly, even as the country time-travelled

into the future in 1982, ten years before I arrived

and ten more before I first encountered an act that could be performed

in all the days that it could occupy. It was written.

Takkan melayu hilang di dunia
Takkan melayu hilang di duni
Takkan melayu hilang di dun
Takkan melayu hilang di du
Takkan melayu hilang di d
Takkan melayu hilang di
Takkan melayu hilang d
Takkan melayu hilang
Takkan melayu hilan
Takkan melayu hila
Takkan melayu hil
Takkan melayu hi
Takkan melayu h
Takkan melayu
Takkan melay
Takkan mela
Takkan mel
Takkan me
Takkan m
Takkan
Takka
Takk
Tak
Ta
T

On the shore she spoke,
and I listened.
We, surrounded by another

archipelago with a history
askew from our own,
hers still told more slant than mine.

Originally from Kedah,

fricative failing the crescendo after years
of needing to speak as another.
Cut the cable and float away.

The boat that evaded the monsoon lash
off another island. The water
that threatened to stopper the close.

What was it they said?

Still I could close
my eyes and imagine
other routes.

II.

What are your responsibilities to a body that wants to write itself out?
>   *It was said that you can only shade yourself in.*

Each day I fumble for a knob that will turn the door into the present and nowhere else.
>   *Where does that lead to?*

What is this body bloated with?
>   *A history.*

The ocean pining for that return.
>   *Who remembers the shore unless there is a storm?*

Why did Nadra feel the pull of another ocean as a low rumble?
>   *She wanted to return to the busiest waterway in the world.*

Resenting things.
>   *Did you resent the fact that you were not told to embrace your own porosity?*

Were you resentful of a history writ large across only one headline?
>   *"The Malays apart, a sense of irrevocable belonging*
>   *to place had yet to develop for a majority of the others."*

Upon the fulcrum of a full lung, I felt the waves of that other life come over me.
>   *Are you ready to absorb everything that the ocean will bring in?*

"Adakah kamu berasa mahu berlayar bagi mendapat peluangan baru?"
>   *Yes.*

To feast on the winds as a measure of.
>   *Can you write clearly, and simply,*
>   *and tell everyone how you could finally arrive?*

       resent this body

its acre of feelings

    false measure

                  legal fiction

          ropes taut

                  meant only for grasping

           penance

                constant splintering

                fruitless bloat

      penance

                useless heft

                fashionable noun

     penance

               con
                    sequences

   this body

                worthy

Where they speak to me in my language as if that could stave off the contemporary.

Where the way back is domestic and emotionally puerile.

Where the way forward continues its arc toward the full comprehension of my adult life.

Where I am taught how I ought to see myself.

Where I enact a suitable pastoral.

Where I meet someone possessed of a different fire, speaking like a ghost.

Where someone else speaks to me and I understand I am not permitted a certain residency.

Where I respond because that's the only way to twist a narrative back into shape.

Where I nudge all the mirrors.

And she wanted to continue the story.
It was not written but she wanted to write it.
The story a story centuries past.
Now tourist trap for where the slipped ship also turned to stone.
N- ow tourist trap for the petrified son groveling by the shore.
Now tourist trap for the son who could not receive his loincloth-swathed mother.
Stones all wrapped up in another story easily swallowed.

Ada suatu lukisan Encik Klee yang dinamakan Angelus Novus. Terlukis seorang malaikat yang lihat seperti beliau mahu menjauhi diri daripada apa yang dilihat. Matanya terbeliak, mulutnya ternganga, dan sayapnya terkedang. Ini adalah rupa sebenar Malaikat Sejarah. Mukanya hanya boleh pandang kepada yang sudah lepas. Manakala kita lihat peristiwa yang ada hikmahnya, beliau hanya menyaksikan Kiamat, yang menghempapkan runtuhan demi runtuhan di telapak kakinya. Dia mahu berhenti sebentar [verweilen], mahu membangunkan mereka yang sudah maut dan mahu menyambungkan apa yang telah dipisahkan. Tetapi ribut Syurga meniup kuat, angin tersangkut di sayapnya; dengan sesungguhnya Malaikat Sejarah pun tidak mampu menutupnya. Ribut ini menolaknya kepada masa depan; belakangnya pandang ke hadapan. Namun runtuhan menambah hingga ke tujuh lapis langit. Yang kita namakan Kemajuan adalah ribut tersebut.

—*Theses on the Philosophy of History*, Walter Benjamin

How much of us is at our mercy?
  The fact of the island was not.
  In spite of everything, the debilitating loneliness.
  This body so badly wishes for home, for a chance to speak, but can find nothing in itself to do so.
  Meanwhile other people attempt to speak.
  In none of them do I find me, but I do find that some of it fits.
  It is no use crying.
  That one took so many tentative steps away should not be a point of mourning.
  I am here because I misspoke.
  What then? Return home?

Kami mahu orang mempunyai rasa tengah, sejarah, cerita yang munasabah. Kami mahu katakan Inilah tingkah lakunya, dan inilah sebabnya. Ia merupakan mangga tahan Azab. Benarkah?

— *Nox*, Anne Carson

Setiap mayat diikuti oleh tiga hal: keluarga, harta dan amalnya. Dua yang pertama kembali pulang, dan yang satu setia mengikut.

— Sahih al-Bukhari 6514

The ledger was complete when She died.

The rollcall of worshippers upwards struck by the sweat clinging to Her rayon, Her chest.

I was told She could not speak at the close.

Then the call.

To the other son and other daughter.

To the children who are told not to look while other children wept.

I was permitted to see the body only later.

At the cusp of another, she brought my brother to watch.

The terms and conditions of her compact are such that one is in eternal preparation

for what is to come.

I can think of at least one way for the dead inside us to re-emerge.

ABOUT THE POETS

Ally Chua is a Singaporean poet. She was the 2019 Singapore Unbound Fellow for New York City and a member of local writing collective /s@ber. Ally has been published in *Quarterly Literary Review Singapore, Cordite Poetry Review*, and *Lammergeier Magazine*.

Andrew Kirkrose Devadason (he/him/his; b. 1997) is a queer transgender Singaporean. Under his birth name, Devadason contributed the winning piece of the 2019 Hawker Prize to the journal *OF ZOOS*. His work has appeared in journals including *Cordite Poetry Review* and *PERVERSE* and in anthologies including *EXHALE: An Anthology of Queer Singapore Voices*.

Anurak Saelaow is a Singaporean poet. His work has been published in *Cha: An Asian Literary Journal, Hayden's Ferry Review, Quarterly Literary Review Singapore, Cultural Weekly, The Kindling, Ceriph*, and elsewhere. He is the author of one chapbook, *Schema* (The Operating System, 2015), and holds a BA in creative writing and English from Columbia University.

Christian Yeo's work has been published in *The Mays, Anthropocene*, and the *Quarterly Literary Review Singapore*, among others. He won the Arthur Sale Poetry Prize, was runner-up for the Aryamati Poetry Prize, and has been shortlisted for the Bridport Prize, the Sykes Prize, and the CUPPS Poetry and Prose Prize. His work has been performed at the Lancaster and Singapore Poetry Festivals.

Hamid Roslan is the author of *parsetreeforestfire* (Ethos Books, 2019). His other work can be found in the *Asian American Writers Workshop, Asymptote, minarets, the Practice Research & Tangential Activities (PR&TA) Journal, The Volta, Of Zoos*, and the *Quarterly Literary Review Singapore*, among others.

ila's (@ilailailailaila_) research centres on peripheral narratives surrounding identity, space and histories that lie hidden, particularly kinship with the land and sea. She writes short speculative prose on @myheartisanelephant, an ongoing project about the city titled "pura-pura parade." She does art sometimes.

Izyanti Asa'ari has been published in anthologies, *Ceriph #3, This is Not a Safety Barrier* (Ethos Books, 2016), and *to let the light in* (SingLit Station, 2021) and is a recipient of the Manuscript Assessment Scheme by National Arts Council Singapore. Her work picks at the stories a city inherits, what makes the machine tick.

Jack Xi (they/he) is a queer, disabled Singaporean poet. A member of the writing collective /Stop@BadEndRhymes (stylised /s@ber), they've appeared in several online poetry journals and Singaporean anthologies and can be found at jackxisg.wordpress.com.

Kenneth Constance Loe (he/they) is an artist, writer, and performer from Singapore, currently based in Vienna, Austria. His practice revolves around material and sensorial fetishes of desire, queer ecologies, and other tangential thoughts through a performative collocation of sculpture, video, text, movement, and olfactory objects.

Laetitia Keok is a writer and editor from Singapore. She is interested in (re)encountering writing as a site of/for collective care and embodied grief. Her work has been nominated for the Pushcart Prize and published in *Hobart Pulp, Wildness Journal, Diode Poetry Journal*, and elsewhere. Find her at laetitia-k.com

Lisabelle Tay is the author of *Pilgrim* (The Emma Press, 2021), which is her debut pamphlet. Her work appears in *Bad Lilies, Crab Creek Review, Strange Horizons*, and elsewhere. She lives in Singapore.

Lune Loh is a core member of /S@BER, a Singaporean writing collective. She graduated from the National University of Singapore in 2022. Her works have appeared in journals and magazines such as *Pank Magazine, Evergreen Review, SOFTBLOW, Cha, Cordite*, and various *SingPoWriMo* issues from 2017–2021. Find her waxing at lune.city.

Mok Zining is obsessed with random things: words, arabesques, sand. *The Orchid Folios* is her first book. Zining lives in Singapore, where she spends most of her free time working on *The Earthmovers*, an essay collection about sand.

Nathaniel Chew (he/him) is a writer, erstwhile linguist, and library human living in Singapore. His collection *featherweight* won the 2019 Golden Point Award for Poetry in English. His writing and writing adjacencies have been published in anthologies by Math Paper Press, Longbarrow Press, Poetry School, and in *QLRS, SingPoWriMo, Pareidolia Literary*, et al.

Shawn Hoo is the author of *Of the Florids* (Diode Editions, 2022). He is Translation Tuesdays Editor at *Asymptote*. Shawn's poems can be found in *New Delta Review, Quarterly Literary Review Singapore, Queer Southeast Asia, Voice & Verse Poetry Magazine*, and his translations in the *Journal of Practice, Research and Tangential Activities* (PR&TA) and *Exchanges: Journal of Literary Translation*.

Shou Jie Eng is a designer, researcher, and writer, whose work examines the relationships between spaces, bodies, and the material histories and cultures of craft. He runs Left Field Projects, a studio practice located in Hartford, CT. His writing has appeared in *Tupelo Quarterly*, *Softblow*, *Speculative Nonfiction*, and *CARTHA*. He teaches at the Rhode Island School of Design in Providence, RI.

worms virk (they/she/he) is a thing-maker, body-shaker, rule-breaker, working primarily through the mediums of art, performance, poetry, prose, and events direction.

ABOUT THE EDITORS

MARYLYN TAN is a sensuous and queer writer-artist-reprobate. Her work aims to subvert, revert, and pervert, to disrespect respectability, to take pleasure seriously, and to reclaim power. Her first child, *GAZE BACK* (Ethos Books, 2018; Singapore Literature Prize, 2020) is the lesbo trans-genre grimoire you never knew you needed.

JEE LEONG KOH is the author of *Steep Tea* (Carcanet), named a Best Book of the Year by UK's *Financial Times* and a Finalist by Lambda Literary in the US. His collection of zuihitsu *The Pillow Book* was shortlisted for the Singapore Literature Prize. His second Carcanet book *Inspector Inspector* was published in August 2022. Originally from Singapore, he lives in New York City.

PERMISSIONS

Ally Chua
"lunar cycle" first appeared in *Salamander* Volume 27.2, "The Boys in the Lineup" first appeared in *opia*, Winter 2021.

Andrew Kirkrose Devadason
"GLASS VASE CELLO CASE" appeared in *minarets*. "The Spare Parts Cycle" appeared in *OF ZOOS*. "TRUTH CONDITIONS" appeared in *SingPoWriMo*.

Anurak Saelaow
"Degustation" appeared in *Singapore Unbound*; "Affidavit Disregarding the Body" appeared in *SingPoWriMo: The Anthology* (2021); "Strategic Sand Reserves" appeared in *Cha: An Asian Literary Journal*.

Christian Yeo
"Colonial Apologist" has appeared in *The Magdalenite*, and "Farm Mart" has appeared in the *Home is Here* anthology and the *CAP Commemorative 30th-Year Anniversary*.

Hamid Roslan
Excerpts from "The Shape of a Body Uncertain" first appeared in *minarets* Issue 12/2021.

ila
"seni itu sunyi" was first presented in the exhibition of Nyanyi Sunyi's Closing Event in 2018 at Gillman Barracks. "Diam-Diam" was commissioned by SingLit Station for #NEVERBEFORESG.

Izyanti Asa'ari
"Parting words" and "The horizon bends" first appeared in *to let the light in* (SingLit Station, 2021). "In the desert, a wolf" was first published in *Ceriph* #3 (2010).

Jack Xi
An earlier version of "This Solidity, of Course, Is What Humankind Yearns for" appeared in *This Concrete Ache* (Yale-NUS Literary Collective, 2021). "A Season of Slime" appeared in *minarets* #12 (Compound Press, 2021). "La Malekzorcismo de la Kvira Korpo" appeared in *Issue 7.1 — Rough Material* (OF ZOOS, 2018) and then *Exhale: An Anthology of Queer Singapore Voices* (Math Paper Press, 2021). An earlier version of "The Merman Dye and Another Man Talking" appeared in *Haunted*, Vol. III (Wyvern Lit, 2018).

Kenneth Constance Loe
Commissioned by Typogaráž, Bratislava, "Pitahaya in Three Parts" appeared in their Autumn '20 programme posters; "it starts with a nip," was shown at the exhibition *FUCK CULTURE, DESCRIPTIVE* as part of the Porn Film Festival Vienna 2021; "Laeken Placid" accompanied the eponymous exhibition at LE KABINET, Brussels, Belgium.

Laetitia Keok
"Maxwell Food Centre (1997)" was first published in *Wildness Journal*; "The Rivers of Us" was first published in *Lumiere Journal*; "Object Permanence" was first published in *Longleaf Review*.

Lisabelle Tay
"Mangosteen Season", "John at the end of his days", and "Three Stars" first appeared in *Bad Lilies* (2022). "Pilgrim" first appeared in *Pilgrim* (The Emma Press, 2021).

Lune Loh
"Sleep Paralysis as Lucid Dreaming" was first published in *SOFTBLOW* (January 2020), "FEMME DIALECTICS: A PROCESS" was first published in *Evergreen Review* (Spring / Summer 2020).

Marylyn Tan
"daddy issues" appeared in *EXHALE: An Anthology of Queer Singapore Voices, Vol 1: Poetry* (Math Paper Press, 2021) and *Rollercoasters & Bedsheets: An Anthology of Sex in Minutes* (Pillow Book Media, 2015). "A WET CRIMSON BUSHEL OF PEARS" appeared in *Voicemail Poems* (2020). "THE OSCAR ROSARY" is forthcoming from Gutslut Press in 2023. "QUEER FILTH INFERNAL" was commissioned for the anthology *Divining Dante* (Recent Work Press, 2021). "CURSING THE FIG TREE: THE HOLY PREPUCE & OTHER DELICIOUS RECIPES" is excerpted from *GAZE BACK* (Ethos Books, 2018), excerpt by Marylyn Tan. *GAZE BACK* © Ethos Books, 2018. Reprinted with permission from the author and Ethos Books, Singapore.

Mok Zining
The following poems were excerpted from *The Orchid Folios* (Ethos Books, 2020): "Floristry Basics: Cuttings," "Floristry Basics: Synonyms," "Exemplary Arrangement C: 'Colonialism: Adaptive Reuse,'" "Lesson on Cuttings: Trimming Unnecessary Affixes," "Exemplary Arrangement C: Background & Discussion Questions," "Bestselling Bouquets: *Vanda* Miss Joaquim Pendant," and "Orchid Basics: Lip Modification." Excerpts by Mok Zining. *The Orchid Folios* © Ethos Books, 2020. Reprinted with permission from the author and Ethos Books, Singapore.

Nathaniel Chew
"language acquisition" was first published in *Crazy Little Pyromaniacs*, eds. Crispin Rodriguez and Andrea Yew (Math Paper Press, 2020). In "pattern recognition," text prefaced with [. . .] is from Jean Berko, "The Child's Learning of English Morphology" (*WORD* 14:2-3, 1958); illustrations by Natalie B. "rag / bone" is written after Robert Zhao Renhui, *Singapore, very old tree*, no. 12, a photo of which is included in the footnote. "after eschatology" was first published in *SingPoWriMo* volume 6 (2020). "scar story" and "pattern recognition" were first published in *Practice, Research and Tangential Activities* (PR&TA) issue 2 (2022).

Shawn Hoo
"Natural History of the Florids, 19th Century," "Natural History of the Florids, 20th Century," "Natural History of the Florids, 21st Century," and "Deferred Sayings for the Next Century" are collected in *Of the Florids* (Diode Editions, 2022), winner of the 2021 Diode Editions Chapbook Prize. The section "Tame" from "Natural History of the Florids, 19th Century" was first published in Vol. 15 No. 1 of *Diode Poetry Journal*. The section "Name" from "Natural History of the Florids, 20th Century" was first published in Issue 11.2 of New Delta Review. "Deferred Sayings for the Next Century" first appeared as "Deferred Sayings for Future Occasions" in Issue 8.1 of *OF ZOOS*. "Placard" was first published in Vol. 20 No. 2 of the *Quarterly Literary Review Singapore*. "Ode to the Public Toilet" was first published in Issue 3.12 of *Queer Southeast Asia: A Literary Journal of Transgressive Art*.

Shou Jie Eng
Sections II, III, V, and VI of "Eight Divers" previously appeared in *Tupelo Quarterly* and *SOFTBLOW*. "How We Build (When We Know How)" was first published as "Hopkins House Condominium Association" in *Speculative Nonfiction*.

worms virk
"20 August 2019, 9.03 p.m." was first published by Checkpoint Theatre as the comic "Milk Teeth" (2021).

ABOUT GAUDY BOY

From the Latin *gaudium*, meaning "joy," Gaudy Boy publishes books that delight readers with the various powers of art. The name is taken from the poem "Gaudy Turnout" by Singaporean poet Arthur Yap, about his time abroad in Leeds, the United Kingdom. Similarly inspired by such diasporic wanderings and migrations, Gaudy Boy brings literary works by authors of Asian heritage to the attention of an American audience and beyond. Established in 2018 as the imprint of the New York City–based literary nonprofit Singapore Unbound, we publish poetry, fiction, and literary nonfiction. Visit our website at www.singaporeunbound.org/gaudyboy.

Winners of the Gaudy Boy Poetry Book Prize
Time Regime, by Jhani Randhawa
Object Permanence, by Nica Bengzon
Play for Time, by Paula Mendoza
Autobiography of Horse, by Jenifer Sang Eun Park
The Experiment of the Tropics, by Lawrence Lacambra Ypil

Fiction and Nonfiction
The Infinite Library and Other Stories, by Victor Fernando R. Ocampo
The Sweetest Fruits, by Monique Truong
And the Walls Come Crumbling Down, by Tania De Rozario
The Foley Artist, by Ricco Villanueva Siasoco
Malay Sketches, by Alfian Sa'at

From Gaudy Boy Translates
Amanat: Women's Writing from Kazakhstan, edited by Zaure Batayeva and Shelley Fairweather-Vega
Ulirát, edited by Tilde Acuña, John Bengan, Daryll Delgado, Amado Anthony G. Mendoza III, and Kristine Ong Muslim
Picking off new shoots will not stop the spring, edited by Ko Ko Thett and Brian Haman

www.ingramcontent.com/pod-product-compliance
Lightning Source LLC
Chambersburg PA
CBHW020734020526
44118CB00033B/582